Achieving Strategic Excellence

Achieving Strategic Excellence

An Assessment of Human Resource Organizations

**Edward E. Lawler III, John W. Boudreau,
and Susan Albers Mohrman**
with Alice Yee Mark, Beth Neilson, and Nora Osganian

Center for Effective Organizations
Marshall School of Business
University of Southern California

*A CEO report of a study funded by the Human Resource Planning Society
and the corporate sponsors of the Center for Effective Organizations*

STANFORD BUSINESS BOOKS
AN IMPRINT OF STANFORD UNIVERSITY PRESS
STANFORD, CALIFORNIA 2006

Stanford University Press
Stanford, California
© 2006 by the Board of Trustees of the Leland Stanford Junior University.

Printed in the United States of America on acid-free, archival-quality paper

Library of Congress Cataloging-in-Publication Data

Lawler, Edward E.
   Achieving strategic excellence : an assessment of human resource organizations / Edward E. Lawler, John W. Boudreau, and Susan Albers Mohrman, with Alice Yee Mark, Beth Neilson, and Nora Osganian.
     p. cm.
   "Center for Effective Organizations, Marshall School of Business, University of Southern California, a CEO report of a study funded by the Human Resource Planning Society and the corporate sponsors of the Center for Effective Organizations."
   Includes bibliographical references.
   ISBN 0-8047-5331-8 (pbk. : alk. paper)
   1. Personnel management.   2. Organizational effectiveness.   I. Boudreau, John W. II. Mohrman, Susan Albers.   III. Mark, Alice Yee.   IV. Neilson, Beth.   V. Osganian, Nora.   VI. Title.
HF5549.L2877   2006
658.3'01—dc22   2005032770

Original Printing 2006

Last figure below indicates year of this printing:
15 14 13 12 11 10 09 08 07 06
Typeset by BookMatters in 10.5/14 Palatino

CONTENTS

TABLES AND EXHIBITS

TABLES

EXHIBITS

PREFACE

This is the Center for Effective Organizations' (CEO) fourth national study of the human resources (HR) function in corporations. Like the previous studies, it is focused on measuring whether the HR function is changing and on gauging its effectiveness. The study focuses on the extent to which the HR function is changing to become an effective strategic partner. It also analyzes how organizations can more effectively manage their human capital. The present study focuses on many of the same corporations that we studied in 1995, 1998, and 2001. Thus, it allows us to compare data from our earlier studies with the data we collected in 2004.

We are deeply indebted to the Human Resource Planning Society for its support of all four of our studies. We would also like to thank the Marshall School of Business of the University of Southern California for its continuing support of the activities of CEO. In addition, we would like to thank the corporate sponsors of CEO for their support of the Center and its mission; their support is vital to the overall success of the Center and is directly responsible for enabling us to do the kind of research reported here.

We would also like to thank Dan Canning, Arienne McCracken, and Anjelica Wright for their help in preparing the manuscript.

THE AUTHORS

Edward E. Lawler III is Distinguished Professor of Business and Director of the Center for Effective Organizations in the Marshall School of Business at the University of Southern California. He has been honored as a major contributor to the fields of organizational development, human resources management, organizational behavior, and compensation. He is the author of over three hundred articles and thirty-eight books. His recent books include *Rewarding Excellence* (Jossey-Bass, 2000), *Corporate Boards: New Strategies for Adding Value at the Top* (Jossey-Bass, 2001), *Organizing for High Performance* (Jossey-Bass, 2001), *Treat People Right* (Jossey-Bass, 2003), *Creating a Strategic Human Resources Organization* (Stanford University Press, 2003), *Human Resources Business Process Outsourcing* (Jossey-Bass, 2004), and *Built to Change* (Jossey-Bass, 2006).

John W. Boudreau, Professor and Research Director at the Marshall School of Business and Center for Effective Organizations at University of Southern California, is recognized worldwide for breakthrough research and consulting that bridges human capital, talent, and sustainable competitive advantage. A Fellow of the National Academy of Human Resources, he has written over fifty books and articles, which have been translated into multiple languages. He has won research awards from the Academy of Management and been featured in *Harvard Business Review*, *The Wall Street Journal*, *Fortune*, and *Business Week*.

Susan Albers Mohrman is a Senior Research Scientist at the Center for Effective Organizations at University of Southern California's Marshall School of Business. Her research, publications, and consulting pertain to knowledge and knowledge-creating organizations, human capital and strategic human resource management, team-based organizations, organizational change and learning with emphasis on the implementation of new designs, and organizational design processes. Her books include *Creating a Strategic Human Resources Organization* (2002, with Edward Lawler). She has served on the Board of Governors of the Academy of Management, and has been a board member of and knowledge partner to the Human Resource Planning Society.

Achieving Strategic Excellence

CHAPTER 1

How HR Can Add Value

Global competition, information technology, new knowledge, the increase in knowledge workers, and a host of other business environment changes are forcing organizations to constantly evaluate how they operate. In many cases they have embraced new strategic initiatives and significantly changed how they operate. They are utilizing new technologies, changing their structures, and improving their work processes to respond to an increasingly demanding and global customer base. These initiatives involve fundamental changes that have significant implications for their human capital and their human resources functions.

Human capital management should be an important part of the strategy of any corporation. The annual reports of many corporations argue that their human capital and intellectual property are their most important assets. In many organizations, compensation is one of the largest, if not the largest, cost. In service organizations compensation often represents 70 to 80 percent of the total cost of doing business. Adding the costs of training and other human resources management activities to the compensation costs, we can see that the human resources function often has responsibility for a large portion of an organization's total expenditures.

But the compensation cost of human capital is not the only, or even the most important, consideration. Even when compensation accounts for very little of the cost of doing business, human capital has a significant impact on the performance of an organization (Cascio, 2000). In essence, without effective human capital, organizations are likely to have little or no revenue. Even the most automated production facilities require skilled, motivated employees to operate them. Knowledge work organizations depend on employees to develop, use, and manage their most important asset, knowledge. Thus, although the human capital of a company does not appear on the balance sheet of corporations, it represents an increasingly large percentage of many organizations' market valuation (Lev, 2001).

A growing body of evidence affirms that HR practices can be a value-added function in an organization. The initial work on the relationship between a firm's performance and its HR practices was conducted by Becker and Huselid (1998). In their study of 740 corporations, they found that firms with the greatest intensity of HR practices that reinforce performance had the highest market value per employee. They argued that HR practices are critical in determining the market value of a corporation and that improvements in HR practices can lead to significant increases in the market value of corporations. They concluded that the best firms are able to achieve both operational and strategic excellence in their HR systems.

Role of the Human Resources Organization

The HR function can add value by adopting a control-and-audit role. But two other roles that it can take on allow it to add still greater value. Lawler (1995) has developed this line of thought by describing the three roles it can take on. The first is the familiar human resources management role (Exhibit 1.1).

The second is the role of business partner (Exhibit 1.2). It emphasizes developing systems and practices to ensure that a company's human resources have the needed competencies and motivation to perform effectively. In this approach, HR has a seat at the table when business issues are discussed and brings an HR perspective to these discussions. When it comes to designing HR systems and practices, this approach focuses on creating systems and practices that support the business strategy. HR also measures the effectiveness of the human capital management practices and focuses on process improvements.

The business partner approach positions the HR function as a value-added part of an organization. It is positioned to contribute to business performance by effectively managing what is the most important capital of most organizations, their human capital. But, this approach may not be one that enables the HR function to add the greatest value. By becoming a strategic partner, HR has the potential to add more value (see Exhibit 1.3).

In acting as a strategic partner, HR plays a role that includes helping the organization develop its strategy. Here, not only does HR have a seat at the strategy table, HR helps to set the table. Boudreau and Ramstad (2005a, 2005b) support this idea by suggesting that strategies can be shaped and enhanced by bringing a human capital decision science to HR's role in strategy.

In the knowledge economy, a firm's strategy must be closely linked to its human talent. Thus, the human resources function must be positioned and designed as a strategic partner that participates in both strategy formulation and implementation. Its expertise in attracting, retaining, developing, deploying, motivating, and organizing human capital is critical to both. Ideally, the HR function should be knowledgeable about the business and expert in organizational and work design issues so that it can help develop needed organizational capabilities and facilitate organizational change as new opportunities become available.

Exhibit 1.1. HR Management

AIMS	Business orientation.
	Services provided expressed as outputs or products.
PROCESS	Build performance management capabilities.
	Develop managers: link competencies to job requirements and career development.
	Succession planning.
	Enhance organizational change capabilities.
	Build an organization-wide HR network.
PLANNING	HR (and all other functions) inspect business plans; inputs from HR may be inserted in the planning process.

Exhibit 1.2. Business Partner

AIMS	Line management owns human resources as a part of their role.
	HR is an integral member of management teams.
	Culture of the firm evolves to fit with strategy and vision.
PROCESS	Organize HR flexibly around the work to be done (programs and projects, outsourcing).
	Focus on the development of people and organizations (road maps, teams, organizational design).
	Leverage competencies, manage learning linkages; build organizational work redesign capabilities.
PLANNING	An integral component of strategic and business planning by the management team.

Exhibit 1.3. Strategic Partner

AIMS	HR is a major influence on business strategy.
	HR systems drive business performance.
PROCESS	Self-service for transactional work.
	Transactional work outsourced.
	Knowledge management.
	Focus on organization development.
	Change management.
	Human resource processes tied to business strategies.
PLANNING	HR is a key contributor to strategic planning and change management.

To be a strategic partner, HR executives need an expert understanding of business strategy, organizational design, and change management, and need to know how integrated human resources practices and strategies can support organizational designs and strategies. This role requires extending HR's focus beyond delivery of HR services and practices to a focus on the quality of decisions about talent, organization, and human capital.

As a strategic partner, HR brings to the table a perspective that is often missing in discussions of business strategy and change—a knowledge of the human capital factors and the organizational changes that are critical to determining whether a strategy can be implemented. Many more strategies fail in execution than in their conception.

Despite compelling arguments supporting human resources management as a key strategic issue in most organizations, human resource executives often are not strategic partners (Lawler, 1995; Brockbank, 1999). All too often, the human resources function is largely an administrative function headed by individuals whose roles are focused on cost control and administrative activities (Ulrich, 1997; Lawler and Mohrman, 2003a; Boudreau and Ramstad, 2005a). Missing almost entirely from the list of HR focuses are key organizational challenges such as improving productivity, increasing quality, facilitating mergers and acquisitions, managing knowledge, implementing change, developing business strategies, and improving the ability of the organization to execute strategies. Since organizations do see these areas as important, the HR function is missing a great opportunity to add value.

There is some evidence that this situation is changing, and that the human resources function is beginning to redefine its role in order to increase the value it adds. The first three phases of the present study (in 1995, 1998, and 2001) found evidence of some change, but notably there was more discussion of change than actual change (Lawler and Mohrman, 2003a).

One possible view of the human resources function of the future is presented in a study of business process outsourcing by Lawler, Ulrich, Fitz-enz, and Madden (2004). It shows how four large corporations (British Petroleum, International Paper, Prudential, and Bank of America) transferred many HR administrative activities to the line, to outside vendors, and to highly efficient processing centers. The HR function was left to focus almost exclusively on business consulting and managing the organization's core competencies. This model is consistent with Ulrich's argument that the HR function needs to be redesigned to operate as a business partner (Ulrich, 1997; Ulrich, Losey, and Lake, 1997). Recently, Ulrich and Brockbank (2005) have argued that the HR function needs to develop a compelling value proposition that focuses on how it can increase the intangible assets that drive the market value of organizations. Boudreau and Ramstad (1997) note that the HR profession could mature in a way similar to finance and marketing.

A number of recent studies have addressed the new competencies required when the human resources function strives to be a strategic business partner (e.g., Smith and Riley, 1994; Csoka, 1995; Eichinger and Ulrich, 1995; Ulrich, 1997; Csoka and Hackett, 1998; Brockbank and Ulrich, 2003). Identifying these competencies needs to be followed by reorganizing the HR function to develop these competencies and to provide services in a manner that adds value as organizations change their overall architecture and strategy.

Creating Change

Describing the new human resources role and the new competencies HR needs is only the first step in transitioning the HR function to a strategic business partner. For decades, the human resources function has been organized and staffed to carry out administrative activities. Changing that role will require a different mix of activities and will necessitate reconfiguring the HR function to support changing business strategies and organizational designs. It also will require the employees in the HR function to have very different competencies than they traditionally have had.

It is becoming increasingly clear that information technology will play a very important role in the future of the HR function (Lawler, Ulrich, Fitz-enz and Madden, 2004). With HR information technology (IT), administrative tasks that have been traditionally performed by the HR function can be done by employees and managers on a self-service basis. Today's HR IT systems simplify and speed up HR activities such as salary administration, job posting and placement, address changes, family changes, and benefits administration; they can handle virtually every administrative HR task. What is more, these systems are available around the clock and can be accessed from virtually anywhere.

Perhaps the greatest value of HR IT systems will result from enabling the integration and analysis of the HR activities. They have the potential to make HR information much more accessible so that it can be used to guide strategy development and implementation. Metrics can be easily tracked and analyses performed that make it possible for organizations to develop and allocate their human capital more effectively (Boudreau and Ramstad, 2006; Lawler, Levenson, and Boudreau, 2004).

A strong case can be made that HR needs to develop much better metrics and analytics capabilities. Our previous three studies identified metrics as one of four characteristics that lead to HR's being a strategic partner. The constituents of HR want measurement systems that enhance their decisions about human capital. All too often, however, HR focuses on the traditional paradigm of delivering HR services quickly, cheaply, and in ways that satisfy clients (Boudreau and Ramstad, 1997, 2003).

HR has become more sophisticated in its measurement, yet this doesn't seem to be leading to increases in organizational effectiveness. Business leaders can now be held accountable for HR measures such as turnover, employee attitudes, bench strength, and performance appraisal distributions; however, this is not the same as creating an effective organization. The issue is how to use HR measures to make a true strategic difference in the organization.

Boudreau and Ramstad (2006) have identified four critical components of a measurement system that drive strategic change and organizational effectiveness: logic, analysis, measures, and process. Measures represent only one component of this system. Though measures are essential, without the other three components they are destined to remain isolated from the true purpose of the HR measurement systems.

Boudreau and Ramstad have also proposed that HR can make great strides by learning how more mature and powerful decision sciences have evolved their measurement systems (Boudreau and Ramstad, 1997). They identify three anchor points—efficiency, effectiveness, and impact—that connect decisions about resources such as money and customers to organizational effectiveness and that can similarly be used to understand HR measurement.

1. *Efficiency* asks, "What resources are used to produce our HR practices?" Typical indicators of efficiency are cost-per-hire and time-to-fill-vacancies.

2. *Effectiveness* asks, "How do our HR policies and practices affect the talent pools and organization structures to which they are directed?" Effectiveness refers to the effects of HR policies and practices on human capacity (a combination of capability, opportunity, and motivation), and the resulting "aligned actions" of the target talent pools. Effectiveness includes trainees' increased knowledge, better-selected applicants' enhanced qualifications or performance ratings of those receiving incentives.

3. *Impact* reflects the hardest question of the three. Impact asks, "How do differences in the quality or availability of different talent pools affect strategic success?" This question is a component of talent segmentation, just as for marketers a component of market segmentation

Creating a Strategic Human Resources Organization

concerns, "How do differences in the buying behavior of different customer groups affect strategic success?"

Today's HR measurement systems largely reflect the question of efficiency (Gates, 2004), though there is some attention to effectiveness as well, through focusing on such things as turnover, attitudes, and bench strength. Rarely do organizations consider impact (such as the relative effect of different talent pools on organizational effectiveness). More important, it is rare that HR measurement is specifically directed toward where it is most likely to have the greatest effect on key talent. Attention to non-financial outcomes and "sustainability" also needs to be increased, because strategic HR can affect these as well (Boudreau and Ramstad, 2005a).

The Emerging HR Decision Science

The majority of today's HR practices, benchmarks, and measures still reflect the traditional paradigm of excellence defined as delivering high-quality HR services in response to client needs. Even as the field advocates more "strategic" HR, it is often defined as delivering the HR services that are important to executive clients (leadership development, competency systems, board governance, etc.). This traditional service-delivery paradigm is fundamentally limited, because it assumes that clients know what they need. Market-based HR and accountability for business results are now recognized as important (Gubman, 2004). However, it often amounts merely to using marketing techniques or business results to assess the popularity of traditional HR services, or their association with financial outcomes.

Fields such as finance have taken a different approach. They have augmented their service delivery paradigm with a "decision science" paradigm, which teaches clients the frameworks to make good choices. Significant improvements in HR decisions will be attained not by applying finance and accounting formulas to HR programs and processes, but rather by learning how these fields evolved into the powerful, decision-supporting functions they are today. Their evolution provides a blueprint for what should be next for HR. The answer lies not just in benchmarking HR in other organizations, but in evolving to be similar to more strategic functions such as finance and marketing.

The marketing decision science enhances decisions about customers. The finance decision science enhances decisions about money. For human capital, a decision science should enhance decisions about organization talent, and those decisions are made both within and outside the HR function. Boudreau and Ramstad have labeled this emerging decision science "talentship," because it focuses on decisions that improve the stewardship of the hidden and apparent talents of current and potential employees (Boudreau and Ramstad, 2005a).

Organization Design

Contributing to effective organizational design is a major domain in which the HR function has the opportunity to add strategic value. Increasingly, the only sustainable competitive advantage is the ability to organize effectively, respond to change, and manage well (Mohrman, Galbraith, and Lawler, 1998; Lawler and Worley, 2006). Confirmation of this statement is provided by Lawler, Mohrman, and Benson's (2001) study of the Fortune 1000, which shows a significant relationship between firm financial performance and the adoption of new management practices designed to increase the capabilities of the firm.

Staff functions, in general, and HR functions, in particular, are under fire in many organizations because they are perceived as controlling rather than adding value, and as not responding to the demands for change that come from operating units. HR functions are being asked to provide expert support to the strategic initiatives of the company and to take advantage of technology, outsourcing, and other approaches to deliver more efficient and responsive services.

Organizational design is increasingly being recognized as a key factor that enables organizations to develop capabilities and, therefore, to perform in ways that produce a competitive advantage. Organizations are adopting design features with an eye to the value they contribute, that is, how they help the organization accomplish its mission (Galbraith, 2002).

All parts of the organization, operating units and staff functions alike, are being redesigned to deliver higher value. For support groups, doing so requires the development of a business model—a value proposition defining what kind of value they will deliver that the company is willing to pay for because it enhances company performance. It also requires them to determine how services can best be delivered.

Two important trends have been noted in organizational design (Mohrman, Galbraith, and Lawler, 1998). The first is recognizing that design is something more than structure, since it includes elements such as management processes, rewards, people systems, information systems, and work processes. These elements must fit with the strategy and with each other for an organization to perform effectively (Waterman, 1982; Nadler, Gerstein, and Shaw, 1992).

The HR organization must think about whether the elements of the design of the HR function indeed do create a high-performance organization—that is, one capable of delivering maximum value while consuming the fewest possible resources. Doing so means concentrating on the way HR organizes to deliver routine transaction services, traditional HR systems development and administration, and strategic business support. HR must think about its own structure, competencies, customer linkages, competency development, management processes, rewards, and information technology to ensure that scarce resources are optimally deployed to deliver value. In addition to making sure the HR function is optimally designed, HR must ensure that it adds value by helping design the company and its various business units.

The second trend is acknowledging that organizational designs involve complex tradeoffs and contingencies. Clearly, one design approach does not fit all organizations. As new business models emerge, new approaches and organizational forms spring up to deal with the complex requirements that organizations must address (Mohrman, Galbraith, and Lawler, 1998). These new models include complex partnerships, globally integrated firms, customer-focused designs, and network organizations. Furthermore, multi-business corporations are recognizing that different businesses exist in different markets and face varying requirements. Consequently, variation in organizational design is increasing, both within multi-business corporations and between businesses (Galbraith, 2002). Thus, for the company and the HR function, one size does not fit all situations. Different organizational forms require different kinds of HR contribution, and thus different HR functional designs and systems.

Design of the HR Function

Organizational design decisions, for HR as well as for companies as a whole, are made in four key areas:

1. Which functions should be centralized and leveraged, and which should be decentralized in order to focus on the unique needs of different parts of the organization? Organizations are combining centralization and decentralization, trying to be big (coordinated) in functions such as purchasing, when there is an advantage to being big; and small (decentralized and flexible) in functions such as new product development, when there are advantages to being small and agile.

2. Which functions should be performed in-house, and which should be outsourced? Companies are outsourcing when they can purchase high-quality services and products more inexpensively or reliably than they can generate them internally.

3. Which functions should be hierarchically controlled, and which should be integrated and controlled laterally? In some areas, orga-

nizations function in a lateral manner, integrating and creating synergies across various parts of the organization, creating cross-functional units to carry out entire processes, and collaborating with suppliers and customers (Mohrman, Cohen, and Mohrman, 1995). Organizations are searching for ways to leverage across business units while setting up organizational and management approaches that give the optimal levels of flexibility and control to various business units.

4. Which processes should be information technology-based? Today, most organizations are wired and have ERP systems that can do a great deal of the administrative work of HR, but is it advantageous to have them do it?

Traditionally HR (and many other staff groups such as information technology) has been organized in a hierarchical manner and HR has seen its mission as designing, administering, and enforcing adherence to HR policies and systems. As a result, HR has been seen as expensive, a necessary evil consuming resources disproportionate to the value that they add to the company. Among the changes in structure and process that are being advocated for staff functions such as HR are the following:

1. Decentralizing business support to operating units in order to increase responsiveness.

2. Contracting with business units for services that are to be delivered, and perhaps even requiring services to be self-funding as a way of ensuring that businesses get only the services that they are willing to pay for and that they see as contributing to business performance.

3. Finding the most efficient way to deliver processing and transactional services, such as creating efficient central services and/or outsourcing.

4. Using information technology to make processes more efficient and to deliver increased value.

5. Participating in cross-unit teams in order to deliver integrated services and/or to partner with customers to increase line ownership over HR systems or to bring the HR perspective to various organizational cross-functional team activities.

6. Creating centers of excellence that provide expert services often in a consulting capacity to the business.

7. Increasing the rotation of people within various staff functions and between staff and line, and having fewer lifelong careers within a narrow staff function, in order to broaden the perspectives of HR staff professionals and increase their awareness of business issues, as well as to increase the depth of understanding of HR issues among line management.

Conclusion

The future of the HR function in organizations is uncertain. On the one hand, if current trends continue it could end up being largely an administrative function that manages an information technology-based HR system and vendors who do most of the HR administrative work. On the other, it could become a driver of organizational effectiveness and business strategy. Many of the key determinants of competitive advantage depend on effective human capital management. More than ever before, the effectiveness of an organization depends on its ability to address issues such as knowledge management, change management, and capability building, which could fall into the domain of the HR function. The unanswered question at this point is whether HR organizations will rise to the occasion.

In order to increase HR's contribution to organizational effectiveness in the future, HR must rethink its basic value proposition, structure, services, and programs in order to address how it can add value in today's economy with its new organizational forms and business strategies. HR faces a formidable challenge just in helping organizations deal with the human issues that are raised by large-scale, strategic change. To face these challenges effectively, human resources has to focus on how it can add value and how it is organized; it must also improve its competencies and in some areas develop new ones.

CHAPTER 2

Research Design   This study focuses on how human resources organizations are changing in response to the strategic and organizational initiatives that businesses are currently undertaking. It examines the extent to which the design and activities of the HR function are *actually* changing by analyzing data from 1995, 1998, 2001, and 2004. We examine the prevalence of practices that are expected to represent the new directions that human resources organizations must take in order to fit with the changes that are occurring in the organizations they serve. We also examine whether these changes are related to the strategic role of HR. Finally, we examine the impact of how the HR function is designed and how it operates on its effectiveness.

This study focuses in depth on eight areas:

1. *HR's Role and Activities*. Because of changes in the business environment it is reasonable to expect that the emphasis that the HR function places on a variety of HR roles and activities may have changed. A major focus of the study is to learn to what extent the HR function is becoming a strategic partner and which organization designs and HR practices are associated with HR being a strategic partner. Of particular concern is whether increased attention to strategic services, such as organization design and development, is affecting the perceived effectiveness of the HR function. We also focus on finding out how much of an increase or decrease there has been in the emphasis on traditional HR activities such as HR planning, compensation, recruitment, selection, and HR information systems. Of particular interest is whether HR is doing less administration and more strategic work.

2. *Decision Science for Talent Resources*. Numerous books and articles that discuss the war for talent have highlighted the fact that organizations are increasingly competing for human capital. They also, of course, need to effectively manage their talent. The present study focuses on whether organizations have developed a decision science for important talent decisions.

3. *The Design of the HR Function*. The study will examine whether changes have occurred in the way the HR function is organized in order to increase the value that it delivers. Because of their role in the balance between efficiency and customer-focused support, we look at the utilization of shared services units and centers

of excellence. We also look at the use of self-service and the presence of HR generalists.

4. *Outsourcing*. Outsourcing is becoming an increasingly popular way to deliver HR services and gain HR expertise. Potentially, it is a way to deal with changes in the demand for HR services as well as a way to control costs. Thus, this study focuses both on how common outsourcing is, and what problems it produces.

5. *Information Technology*. HR IT systems can potentially radically change the way HR services are delivered and managed. Thus, the present study examines how companies are using information technology in their HR functions. It looks in detail at the functions that are being done on a self-service basis, and at the effectiveness of HR IT systems with respect to such activities as salary planning, performance management, and new-hire orientation. It also focuses on how effective organizations consider their HR IT systems to be in influencing employee satisfaction and loyalty and providing strategic information.

6. *Metrics and Analytics*. It is important to know both what measures HR organizations are collecting and how they analyze them. Thus, the study looks at both metrics collection and utilization, including the use of score cards and benchmarks. Finally, it looks at how effectively metrics and analytics are being used.

7. *HR Skills*. Critical to the effectiveness of any HR function are the skills of the HR professionals and staff. Thus, the present study examines how satisfied organizations are with their HR professionals' skills in a variety of areas. It particularly focuses on the skills needed in order for HR professionals to serve as true business and strategic partners.

8. *HR Effectiveness*. The effectiveness of the HR function is a critical issue. Particular emphasis in the present study is on the effectiveness of the HR function in doing many of the new activities that are required in order for HR to be a business and strategic partner. These include managing change, contributing to strategy, managing the outsourcing of HR, and operating shared service units. Perhaps the crucial issue with respect to effectiveness concerns the practices that lead to an effective HR organization. Thus, the present study focuses on what HR structures, approaches, and practices are associated with effectiveness in an HR organization.

Sample

This is the fourth study in a series examining whether there is change in the human resources organizations of large- and medium-sized corporations. In the first study, in 1995, surveys were mailed to HR executives at the director level or above in 417 large- and medium-sized service and industrial firms (Mohrman, Lawler, and McMahan, 1996). The executives chosen had broad visibility to the human resource function across the corporation. Responses were received from 130 companies (response rate 19.6 percent). The second study, done in 1998, mailed surveys to similar executives in 663 similar firms, with 119 usable surveys returned (response rate 17.9 percent) (Lawler and Mohrman, 2000). In the third study, done in 2001, 996 surveys were mailed, and 150 usable surveys were received (15.5 percent response rate) (Lawler and Mohrman, 2003a).

In the present (2004) study, surveys were mailed, again to HR executives with corporate visibility of the HR function in large and medium-sized companies.

In all four studies, a three-step data collection procedure was used. In August 2004, surveys were mailed. Four weeks after the initial mailing, reminder letters were mailed to all firms that had not returned completed surveys. Sixty days later, a second questionnaire was sent to firms who had not yet responded. A total of 100 usable surveys were returned by executives, for a response rate of 11.1 percent. A complete copy of the 2004 survey with frequencies and means for each item appears as Appendix A.

For the first time in 2004, data were collected from non-HR senior managers. Three copies of a manager's survey were mailed along with the HR survey to each HR executive. A cover letter to the HR executive asked that the survey be distributed to individuals who were not in HR, but were in a position to evaluate the function. At least one manager questionnaire was received from 77 companies. A complete copy of the 2004 manager survey with frequencies and means can be found in Appendix B. When multiple responses were received from a company, a mean response for the company was computed and used in all the data analyses.

Measures

The 2004 HR survey is an expanded version of the three previous surveys. It covers eleven general areas:

1. General descriptive information about the demographics of the firm and the human resources function.

2. The organizational context that the human resources function serves, including its broad organizational form and the amount and kinds of strategic change and organizational initiatives being carried out by the company.

3. The changing focus of the human resources function measured in terms of how much time it is spending in different kinds of roles compared with five to seven years ago.

4. The degree of emphasis that a number of human resources activities are receiving and the involvement of HR in business strategy.

5. Human resources' use of various organizational practices to increase efficiency and business responsiveness and the extent to which human resources is investing in a number of strategic initiatives to support strategic change.

6. The use of outsourcing and the problems that have been encountered in using it (new in 1998).

7. The use of information technology and its effectiveness (new in 1998, expanded in 2001).

8. The use of HR metrics and analytics as well as their effectiveness (new in 2004).

9. How HR leaders and business leaders make decisions that involve human capital (new in 2004).

10. The changing skill requirements for employees in the HR function and satisfaction with current skills.

11. The perceived effectiveness of the human resources function and the importance of a variety of HR activities.

The findings will be reported in roughly this order.

Staffing of Human Resources Function

In the firms studied, the average number of employees in the human resources function was 307. This represents a significant decrease from 1998, when the number was 402, and from the 1995 number of 377. It is larger than 2001, when it was 234. The ratio of total employees to HR employees was 100 to 1. This ratio is higher than the 2001 ratio of 90 to 1, the 1998 ratio of 87 to 1, and the 1995 ratio of 92 to 1.

The ratio of HR staffing in this study is generally in line with those found in other studies. For example, the 2000/2001 BNA survey reports a ratio of 100 to 1 (BNA, 2001). This is essentially the same ratio they found in their 1996 survey. Thus, despite the introduction of information technology and the downsizing of corporate staff groups, there is no dramatic decrease in the size of the HR function relative to the rest of the organization. Why this is true is unclear at this point. It may reflect the increased importance of the function or simply that HR is a well-institutionalized part of most organizations that is difficult to reduce in size.

Information on staffing of the HR function for the firms responding to the study is in Table 2.1. Of the total human resources staff in these organizations, 48 percent were described as generalists, a slight increase

Table 2.1. HR Generalists and Specialists

Percentage of Human Resources Employees	1995	1998	2001	2004
HR generalist	46	46	43	**48**
Corporate staff	44	43	46	**38**

N = 100 as of 1/5/05.

from previous years. Thirty-eight percent of the human resources professional/managerial staff were part of a centralized corporate staff function, down somewhat from the previous years, when between 43 and 46 percent were part of a centralized corporate staff function.

Companies in the survey typically operated in several countries. In the companies that operated internationally, 24.1 percent of their HR professionals were located outside the United States, whereas 30.5 percent of their employees were outside the United States. This suggests that to some degree there is less staffing of the HR function outside of the United States than inside the United States, undoubtedly because some corporate services from the United States are provided to employees in other countries. This finding is consistent with the results of the 2001 survey.

The respondents were asked to state the background of the current head of human resources. In 77.9 percent of cases, the top human resources executive came up through the human resources function. In the other 22.1 percent of cases, these executives came from functions including operations, sales and marketing, and legal. This result is similar to findings of the 2001 survey.

Why do some firms continue to place executives in charge of the human resources function who are not "traditional" human resources executives? There are three likely reasons. First, senior executives without an HR background are being put in charge of HR in order to develop them because they are candidates for the CEO job. Second, they are being put in charge of HR in order to make HR run more like a business and be more of a business partner. Third, failed line managers are being put into HR because it is seen as a "safe" pre-retirement job. The survey did not ask why this is done, so we can only speculate that in the majority of cases it is done in order to change the HR function or to develop an executive. In today's business world it usually is too important a position to use as a "dumping" ground.

Organizational Forms

Most organizations start out with simple structures and offer only a small number of products and services that serve a defined market. They have small staff groups and are organized around functions such as sales and manufacturing. They are often small enough to operate largely through informal coordination. As organizations grow and the number of products, services, and markets increase, informal coordination is no longer adequate. The structure grows in complexity and formality as the organization goes through phases of growth. If the company relies on one major set of technologies and a set of related products that can be developed, marketed, and distributed in similar ways, the company may retain a functional form (Mohrman, Galbraith, and Lawler, 1998). When this happens, a centralized human resource function typically provides services to the organization.

If the company grows through increasing the variety of its products and services and the diversity of its markets and distribution channels, it may divide into multiple business units, each of which is, itself, a complete, multifunctional structure. As long as these business units are related, perhaps because they rely on common technology, serve similar customers, or distribute through a common channel, companies usually have a centralized HR function. Here, the HR challenge is to organize the function to allow businesses to pursue their unique needs and strategies while providing economies of scale and a foundation for integration across the businesses where it is desirable.

When a company diversifies to the extent that it houses a number of quite different businesses that have different markets, technologies, and distribution channels, it usually is organized into groups or sectors, each of which houses a number of related businesses. When this occurs, the opportunities for synergy among groups are limited. Nevertheless, a company may continue to add value by organizing some activities, such as HR, on a corporation-wide basis. Alternatively, a company may choose to manage its businesses as a financial portfolio only, and may adopt a holding company form that has little or no corporate staff. In this approach, each business unit has its own HR staff.

Table 2.2 shows the breakdown of the 1995, 1998, 2001, and 2004 samples of companies on the basis of their structure. By far the largest group of companies in all of the studies are those with multiple, related business units. Single integrated businesses and corporations with multiple sectors or groups of businesses comprise the remainder of the sample. The table also shows the number of companies that are considered large sized, that is, having more than 20,000 employees. Organizational size is important to consider because it often influences how corporate staff groups, such as HR, are structured and operated. Almost half of the companies in this study's sample have more than 20,000 employees.

Costs may be reduced by creating corporate HR groups for services that do not require business-specific adaptation. It may also be optimized by

Table 2.2. Organizational Structure

	Single Integrated Business	Multiple Related Business	Several Sector Businesses	Multiple Unrelated Businesses	Large Companies
2004 Percentages	**22.4**	**53.1**	**21.4**	**1.0**	**47.5**
2001 Percentages	25.7	38.5	26.4	5.4	32.0
1998 Percentages	23.5	49.6	26.1	0	47.9
1995 Percentages	29.1	40.9	26.0	1.6	44.5

decentralizing or outsourcing the provision of services that need to be tailored to particular operating units.

Each of the three major forms of organization that are represented in our sample face common decisions about how to organize human resources and other support functions. They must decide how much commonality and integration of practice they want across business units, and how much they want to organize to achieve economies of scale. These objectives have to be weighed against the objectives of delivering services that are tailored for each part of the organization and that are delivered in a manner which supports flexibility and optimization at the business-unit level. In companies that have multiple businesses, this balance has to be very carefully weighed in designing for optimal Human Resource contribution.

The Strategic and Organizational Context

Human resource organizations exist in organizational environments that are as turbulent as the competitive environments in which companies find themselves. As companies take measures to survive and prosper, they make changes and introduce initiatives that change the organization, the competencies it has, the way it manages its human resources, and its expectations of and relationships to its employees (Lawler, 1995; Lawler, Mohrman, and Benson, 2001). Thus, in order to understand an HR function it is important to examine how its characteristics are related to its organization's strategic focuses.

Table 2.3 shows the prevalence of a number of strategic focuses that are often part of a company's business strategy. It also shows that the items measuring strategic focus factor into six types of focus: growth, knowledge, information, core business, quality and speed, and organizational performance. The items concerned with knowledge, information, and quality and speed are the most prevalent. The item on customer focus is the most prevalent single strategic focus. The least prevalent focus is strategies involving changes to the core business.

Table 2.3. Strategic Focuses

Strategic Focus	1995	1998	2001	2004
Growth	—	—	—	**3.0**
Building a global presence	3.4	3.2	3.0	2.9
Acquisitions	2.8	3.5	3.1	2.9[1]
Expansion into new markets	—	—	—	3.2
Core business	—	—	—	**2.2**
Partnering/networking with other companies	2.9	2.8	3.1	2.7
Reducing the number of businesses you are in	—	1.9	1.9	1.7
Exiting businesses	—	—	—	2.0
Quality and speed	**3.7**	**3.5**	**3.7**	**3.6**
Cycle time reduction	3.5	3.4	3.4	3.3
Accelerating new product innovation	3.7	3.5	3.7	3.4
Quality	3.9	3.6	3.9	4.1[1]
Information-based strategies	—	—	—	**3.5**
Customer focus	—	4.4	4.4	4.4
Process automation/information technology	—	3.9	3.8	3.7
Technology leadership	—	3.6	3.5	3.4
e-Business	—	—	3.2	2.6
Knowledge-based strategies	—	—	—	**3.4**
Talent – being an employer of choice	—	—	3.8	3.7
Knowledge / intellectual capital management	—	2.9	2.9	3.1
Human capital strategy for competitive advantage	—	—	—	3.3
Organizational performance	—	—	—	**3.1**
Cost leadership	—	—	—	3.3
Total quality management / six sigma	3.4	2.8	2.5	2.7
Employee involvement	3.4	3.5	3.2	3.3

Response scale: 1 = little or not extent; 2 = some extent; 3 = moderate extent; 4 = great extent; 5 = very great extent

Note: Items with (—) were not asked.

[1] Significant difference ($p \leq .05$) between 1998 and 2004.

On balance, these data support the point that organizations exist in dynamic environments and have in place a variety of strategic and organizational initiatives to better position themselves to perform successfully. The human resource function, if it is to add value and act as a strategic partner, needs to help ensure that the organizational capabilities and competencies exist to cope with a dynamic environment. In order to determine how it is coping, we will look not only at how the human resource function is changing, but also at how changes in it are being driven by companies' strategies.

CHAPTER 3

Role of Human Resources

A key issue for HR functions is how they spend their time. They are responsible for a number of administrative activities and services; in addition, they can do higher value-added business partner and strategic work.

Respondents were asked to estimate the percentage of time that the human resources function currently spends in carrying out a number of roles and how much time was spent on them five to seven years ago. Table 3.1 shows that the respondents report that the function spends the most time on service provision. They also report that there has been significant change in how time is spent over the last five to seven years. According to the HR executives, currently less time is being spent on record-keeping, auditing, and service provision, and more time on the development of new HR systems and practices and on being a strategic business partner.

Overall, our respondents report significant movement toward HR becoming a strategic partner and doing higher value-added activities. However, before we conclude that this has actually occurred it is important to look at the results from 1995, 1998, and 2001.

The data from 1995, 1998, and 2001 are almost identical to the data collected in 2004 when the same question was asked (see Tables 3.2, 3.3, and 3.4). There is no change in the current time responses or in the responses concerning five to seven years ago. This finding raises two interesting points. First, it means that there has been little change in the last nine years in terms of how HR executives report the HR function spends its time when they report on their current activities. Second, it raises serious questions about the validity of the reports by our respondents about how things were five to seven years ago.

It might be expected that the 2004 estimates of how things were five to seven years earlier would be somewhat in line with how things were said to be in our 1995 study, in our 2001 study, and especially in our 1998 study (six years ago), but they are not. Instead, rather than there being a change in time spent, the 1995, 1998, and 2001 results are the same as the results for 2004! This finding suggests that the HR executives who responded in 2004, as well as those that responded in 1995, 1998, and 2001, may have perceived more change in their role than has actually taken place. In short, they may be guilty of wishful thinking.

What should we believe, retrospective reports of the way things were,

Table 3.1. Percentage of Time Spent on Various Human Resources Roles (2004)

Role	Means		
	5 to 7 Years Ago	Current	Difference
Maintaining Records Collect, track, and maintain data on employees	25.9	13.2	Significant Decrease
Auditing/Controlling Ensure compliance to internal operations, regulations, and legal and union requirements	14.8	13.3	Significant Decrease
Human Resources Service Provider Assist with implementation and administration of HR practices	36.4	32.0	Significant Decrease
Development of Human Resources Systems and Practices Develop new HR systems and practices	12.6	18.1	Significant Increase
Strategic Business Partner As a member of the management team, involved with strategic HR planning, organizational design, and strategic change	9.6	23.5	Significant Increase

Table 3.2. Percentage of Time Spent on Various Human Resources Roles (2001)

Role	Means		
	5 to 7 Years Ago	Current	Difference
Maintaining Records Collect, track, and maintain data on employees	26.8	14.9	Significant Decrease
Auditing/Controlling Ensure compliance to internal operations, regulations, and legal and union requirements	17.1	11.4	Significant Decrease
Human Resources Service Provider Assist with implementation and administration of HR practices	33.1	31.3	No Significant Change
Development of Human Resources Systems and Practices Develop new HR systems and practices	13.9	19.3	Significant Increase
Strategic Business Partner As a member of the management team, involved with strategic HR planning, organizational design, and strategic change	9.1	23.2	Significant Increase

Table 3.3. Percentage of Time Spent on Various Human Resources Roles (1998)

Role	Means		
	5 to 7 Years Ago	Current	Difference
Maintaining Records Collect, track, and maintain data on employees	25.6	16.1	Significant Decrease
Auditing/Controlling Ensure compliance to internal operations, regulations, and legal and union requirements	16.4	11.2	Significant Decrease
Human Resources Service Provider Assist with implementation and administration of HR practices	36.4	35.0	No Significant Change
Development of Human Resources Systems and Practices Develop new HR systems and practices	14.2	19.2	Significant Increase
Strategic Business Partner As a member of the management team, involved with strategic HR planning, organizational design, and strategic change	9.4	20.3	Significant Increase

Table 3.4. Percentage of Time Spent on Various Human Resources Roles (1995)

Role	Means		
	5 to 7 Years Ago	Current	Difference
Maintaining Records Collect, track, and maintain data on employees	22.9	15.4	Significant Decrease
Auditing/Controlling Ensure compliance to internal operations, regulations, and legal and union requirements	19.5	12.2	Significant Decrease
Human Resources Service Provider Assist with implementation and administration of HR practices	34.3	31.3	Significant Decrease
Development of Human Resources Systems and Practices Develop new HR systems and practices	14.3	18.6	Significant Increase
Strategic Business Partner As a member of the management team, involved with strategic HR planning, organizational design, and strategic change	10.3	21.9	Significant Increase

or data from the past about the way things were at the time the data were collected? The answer is obvious: individuals are much better at reporting how things are now than what they were like years ago. Reports of the past often include changes that reflect favorably on the individual. In this case, it is possible that HR executives want to see themselves as more of a strategic partner now than they were in the past. This possibility is quite likely, given the many books and articles which have called for this to happen.

What is surprising is the complete lack of change in current time spent; the results from 1995 are almost identical to those from 2004. Although the world of business has changed a lot since 1995, how HR spends its time has not. HR also continues to believe it has changed, even though it has not!

The relationship between the strategic focuses and how HR spends its time is shown in Table 3.5. The correlations in the table show a clear pattern. Maintaining records, auditing/controlling, and providing services are negatively related to almost all the strategic focuses. Apparently, the weaker an organization's strategic focus, the more the HR function spends its time maintaining records, auditing/controlling, and providing HR services.

Time spent on strategic business partnering by the HR function was found to be strongly related to five of the six strategic focuses. This finding suggests that HR becomes much more involved in strategic business partnering when the organization has a clear strategic focus, regardless of what that focus is. One implication of this finding is that in order for

Table 3.5. Relationship of Strategic Focuses to HR Roles

Role	Strategic Focuses					
	Growth	Core Business	Quality and Speed	Information-Based Strategies	Knowledge-Based Strategies	Organizational Performance
Maintaining Records	-.22*	-.20^t	-.14	-.07	-.31**	-.29**
Auditing/Controlling	-.08	-.13	-.02	.19^t	-.10	.11
Providing HR Services	-.09	-.06	-.28**	-.12	-.09	-.12
Developing HR Systems	.13	.06	.08	.00	.09	.01
Strategic Business Partnering	.23*	.24*	.39***	.07	.32**	.26*

Significance level: ^{t} $p \leq 0.10$ * $p \leq 0.05$ ** $p \leq 0.01$ *** $p \leq 0.001$

HR to become more strategic, organizations themselves may need to become more strategic. Of course, one alternative is for HR to provide leadership and help the rest of an organization become more strategic. If it can accomplish this, we believe there is a good chance HR can spend more time on strategy.

CHAPTER 4

Business Strategy

The involvement that the HR function has in the strategy development and implementation process—how much and what kind—is a key issue. Strategy is an area where human capital concerns need to be given important consideration and it represents a high value-added activity for the HR function.

Type of Involvement

The involvement of the HR function in business strategy can take a variety of forms. Table 4.1 shows that in 2004, virtually all HR executives reported that their function is involved in business strategy. However, in over 60 percent of the companies studied, HR is less than a full partner in the eyes of their HR executives. When 2004 data are compared to those of 1998 and 2001, there is no statistically significant change in the extent to which HR reports being involved in business strategy. Thus, the data do not suggest that the HR function is becoming more of a strategic partner in most organizations.

Managers not in the HR function (from here on we will refer to them as managers) report lower levels of strategic involvement on the part of the HR function than are reported by their counterparts in HR. As can be seen in Table 4.1, only 24 percent of managers see HR as a full partner in developing and implementing the business strategy, compared to 40 percent of HR executives who self-report that they are.

The finding of a difference between HR managers and managers outside of HR is not surprising, in the light of an earlier study that asked HR executives and line managers about the role of HR (SHRM, 1998); it, too, found a significant difference between HR executives and managers in the estimate of the role HR plays in business. Not surprisingly, HR executives saw themselves as more of a business partner than did managers: 79 percent of HR executives said they were business partners, whereas only 53 percent of the managers shared this view.

The differences between HR executives and managers can be explained in a number of ways, among them the fact that HR executives have much greater visibility with respect to their role in strategy than do most managers. Because HR executives have more information, they may have a more accurate image of what their role is in the strategy process.

There is also the possibility that HR executives tend to give themselves

Table 4.1. HR's Role In Strategy

Role in Strategy	All Companies		2004	
	1998	2001	HR Executives	Managers
No Role	4.2	3.4	**2.0**	**5.3**
Implementation Role	16.8	11.6	**12.2**	**18.4**
Input Role	49.6	43.8	**45.9**	**52.6**
Full Partner	29.4	41.1	**39.8**	**23.7**
Mean	3.0	3.2	**3.2**	**2.9**[1]

Means; response scale: 1 = no role to 4 = full partner

[1] Significant difference ($p \leq .05$) between HR executives and managers in 2004.

Table 4.2. Strategic Focuses and HR's Role in Strategy

Role in Strategy	Strategic Focuses					
	Growth	Core Business	Quality and Speed	Information-Based Strategies	Knowledge-Based Strategies	Organizational Performance
No Role	2.5	1.5	3.3	3.1	2.0	2.8
Implementation Role	2.5	2.1	3.5	3.5	3.1	2.8
Input Role	3.1	2.2	3.5	3.5	3.3	3.1
Full Partner	3.0	2.1	3.7	3.6	3.6 [1]	3.3

Means; response scale: 1 = little or no extent; 2 = some extent; 3 = moderate extent; 4 = great extent; 5 = very great extent

[1] Significant difference ($p \leq .05$) for role in strategy

a more important role than they in fact play. The same type of difference might very well appear with any function that is studied. Marketing and finance executives, for example, may see themselves as playing a greater strategic role than would individuals not in those functions. Thus, HR executives may simply be doing what most people do—overestimating their importance. Still, it is important for HR executives to realize that other managers may not share their view of the role the HR function plays in corporate business strategy.

The role that HR plays in the strategy process does appear to be related to the strategic focuses of the organization. As can be seen in Table 4.2, when HR plays an important role in strategy, the general trend is for all of the strategic focuses to be somewhat higher. When an organization has a strategy that is related to knowledge, it is particularly likely to have HR as a full strategic partner.

Strategy Activities

HR can make a number of specific contributions to the strategy process in a business. Some involve implementation, while others involve the development of strategy. Table 4.3 presents the data from a question that was designed to identify the specific activities that HR engages in with respect to business strategy. Not surprisingly, according to HR executives, the thing they are most likely to do by a wide margin with respect to strategy is to recruit and develop talent. At the other extreme is identifying new business opportunities: apparently, this rarely happens.

After the development of talent, the greatest level of activity concerns the implementation of strategy. HR executives report that they are particularly likely to be involved in designing an organization's structure and in planning for the implementation of strategy. This is a logical area of involvement for HR, and it is hardly surprising that this is rated as a major involvement area for HR.

Perhaps the best summary of the results is that HR is more likely to play a role in the implementation of business strategy than in the development of it or making key option decisions concerning it. Finally, it is worth noting that HR is not likely to be involved with the corporate board in discussions of business strategy nor in identifying new business opportunities.

Table 4.3 also shows how managers rate the involvement of HR in business strategy. The results here are consistent with the earlier finding that managers in general tend to see less involvement of HR in strategy than HR executives do. All but one of the items are rated lower by managers than by HR executives. However, only two of the differences reach statistical significance.

Overall, it seems that managers simply do not see HR as involved in business strategy as do HR executives, even when it comes to such specifics as recruiting and developing talent. It is interesting that the relative degree of involvement in different activities as seen by managers and HR executives is very similar. Managers agree with HR executives that the major involvement of HR executives is in recruiting and developing talent and other implementation issues that are involved in strategy. They also agree that HR has little involvement in identifying new business opportunities.

Creating a Strategic Human Resources Organization

Table 4.3. Business Strategy Activities

Strategy Activities	HR Executives		Managers	
	Mean	Correlation with HR Role in Strategy	Mean	Correlation with HR Role in Strategy
Help identify or design strategy options	2.9	.56***	2.7	.65***
Help decide among the best strategy options	3.0	.68***	2.9	.51***
Help plan the implementation of strategy	3.6	.59***	3.4	.33**
Help design the criteria for strategic success	3.2	.68***	2.9	.45***
Help identify new business opportunities	2.0	.57***	2.0	.55***
Assess the organization's readiness to implement strategies	3.5	.65***	3.4	.40***
Help design the organization structure to implement strategy	3.8	.65***	3.5	.31**
Assess possible merger, acquisition or divestiture strategies	2.9	.47***	2.3[1]	.18
Work with the corporate board on business strategy	2.6	.62***	2.5	.50***
Recruit and develop talent	4.6	.38***	4.2[1]	.23*

Response scale: 1 = little or no extent; 2 = some extent; 3 = moderate extent; 4 = great extent; 5 = very great extent

[1] Significant difference ($p \leq 0.05$) between HR executives and managers in 2004.

Significance level: [t] $p \leq 0.10$ * $p \leq 0.05$ ** $p \leq 0.01$ *** $p \leq 0.001$

Table 4.3 also shows the relationship between the business strategy activities and HR's role in strategy. Not surprisingly, the relationships are strong, which indicates that these activities are associated with the degree of involvement HR has in the strategy process. The weakest relationship for HR executives and the second weakest for managers is with recruitment and development of talent. One way of interpreting this finding is that talent management is an activity that HR does regardless of how involved it is in the strategy process. As a result, the degree to which it is involved with other activities may hold the key to HR's becoming stronger as a strategic partner.

There are numerous significant relationships between the company strategic focus areas and the role that HR plays in the strategy process. Two of the strategic focuses, on knowledge-based strategies and on organizational performance, are strongly associated with HR's active involvement in seven of the ten business strategy activities listed in Table 4.4. Both of these focuses show relatively low relationships to working with the board, assessing mergers, and planning strategy implementation, three strategy activities which generally tend to have a low relationship to all of the strategic focuses.

Table 4.4. Relationship of Business Strategy Activities to Strategic Focuses

Strategy Activities	Strategic Focuses					
	Growth	Core Business	Quality and Speed	Information-Based Strategies	Knowledge-Based Strategies	Organizational Performance
Help identify or design strategy options	.13	.10	.25*	.19^t	.23*	.30**
Help decide among the best strategy options	.11	.08	.24*	.19^t	.22*	.26*
Help plan the implementation of strategy	.15	.22*	.18^t	.12	.15	.16
Help design the criteria for strategic success	.11	.10	.31**	.21*	.26**	.19^t
Help identify new business opportunities	.00	.11	.18^t	.25*	.32**	.30**
Assess the organizations readiness to implement strategies	.11	.26*	.19^t	.09	.41***	.35***
Help design the organization structure to implement strategy	.14	.21*	.21*	-.07	.29**	.26*
Assess possible merger, acquisition or divestiture strategies	.16	.31**	-.10	.07	.19^t	.20*
Work with the corporate board on business strategy	.05	.06	.06	.17	.19^t	.15
Recruit and develop talent	.27**	.00	.32***	.12	.43***	.25*

Significance level: ^{t} $p \le 0.10$ * $p \le 0.05$ ** $p \le 0.01$ *** $p \le 0.001$

The strategic focus on growth has the weakest relationship to the strategy activities of the HR function. Not surprisingly, it is significantly related to recruiting and developing talent, since with growth, talent becomes a particularly critical issue.

Three strategic focuses—core business, quality and speed, and information—show significant relationships to only some HR strategy activities. In total, the results on strategic focuses suggest that almost regardless of the strategic focus in an organization, there are HR strategy activities that are relevant and important.

Role in Strategy

Further data on HR's role in strategy are presented in Table 4.5, which contains data both on the current level of HR activity in the strategy area and on future intentions. With respect to the current level of activ-

Creating a Strategic Human Resources Organization

Table 4.5. HR Strategy

HR Strategy Activity	Current Mean	Correlation with HR Role in Strategy	Future Mean	Correlation with HR Role in Strategy
Data-based talent strategy	2.7	.22*	2.5	.16
Partner with line in developing business strategy	3.3	.64***	2.7	.50***
A human capital strategy that is integrated with business strategy	3.2	.43***	2.7	.38***
Provides analytic support for business decision-making	2.9	.43***	2.5	.27**
Provides HR data to support change management	3.2	.45***	2.5	.41***
HR drives change management	3.4	.57***	2.6	.47***
Makes rigorous data based decisions about human capital management	2.7	.37***	2.5	.34***

Current: mean; response scale: 1 = little or not extent, 2 = some extent, 3 = moderate extent, 4 = great extent, 5 = very great extent

Future: mean; response scale: 1 = not in our plans, 2 = possible focus, 3 = an important future focus

Significance level: $^t p \leq 0.10$ $^* p \leq 0.05$ $^{**} p \leq 0.01$ $^{***} p \leq 0.001$

ity, none of the mean scores are particularly high. The highest is 3.4 on a 5-point scale. It appears that to a moderate extent, HR partners with the line in developing a business strategy, drives change management, develops a human capital strategy that is integrated with business strategy, and provides HR data to support change management. HR managers are less active in the use of data and analytics. Data-based decision-making about human capital and data-based talent strategies are the lowest-rated HR activities.

The responses for future activity levels indicate that a role in all of the strategy activities is in the future plans of HR. All of the HR strategy items are rated near the top of the scale (2.5 or greater on a 3-point scale) in terms of the future focus of the HR organization. Apparently, these items represent the way that HR plans to be involved in the strategy process. This includes plans to increase the use of data-based approaches and analytics in developing strategy.

The correlations between the current activity levels and HR's role in strategy are presented in Table 4.5, and they are all high, with one exception. Data-based talent strategies are not particularly highly correlated with HR's current role in strategy. It is not entirely clear why

Table 4.6. Relationship of HR Strategy to Strategic Focuses

HR Strategy Activity	Strategic Focuses					
	Growth	Core Business	Quality and Speed	Information-Based Strategies	Knowledge-Based Strategies	Organizational Performance
Data-based talent strategy	.11	.11	$.18^t$	.15	.27**	.26**
Partner with line in developing business strategy	.20*	.23*	.27**	.17	.43***	.33***
A human capital strategy that is integrated with business strategy	.21*	.14	.21*	.30**	.51***	.35***
Provides analytic support for business decision-making	$.20^t$	.23*	-.03	.16	.31**	$.19^t$
Provides HR data to support change management	.23*	.22*	.15	$.19^t$	.38***	.33***
HR drives change management	.28**	.13	.32***	.27**	.47***	.23*
Makes rigorous data-based decisions about human capital management	.25*	.22*	.25*	.24*	.31**	.23*

Significance level: $^t p \leq 0.10$ $^* p \leq 0.05$ $^{**} p \leq 0.01$ $^{***} p \leq 0.001$

this relationship is so weak, given that it is potentially an important part of the strategy process.

At this point, it appears that an organization's emphasis on data-based talent strategies is relatively independent of HR's role in the general strategy process. This conclusion is further substantiated by the data on future HR strategy activities. On the one hand, there is a weak relationship between the future use of a data-based talent strategy and HR's current role in strategy. On the other hand, all the other HR strategy items are strongly related to HR's future role in strategy.

Table 4.6 shows the relationship between HR strategy roles and the strategic focuses of the organization. There are a number of significant relationships, reinforcing the point that if an organization has a clear strategic focus, HR is likely to also be actively engaged in the strategy area. Perhaps the most interesting finding in the table is the pattern of strong correlations between knowledge-based strategies and the HR strategy items. It is clear that when an organization has a knowledge-based strategy, it particularly emphasizes the role of HR processes and

Creating a Strategic Human Resources Organization

measures in its work. This finding is a further confirmation of the future importance of HR strategic activities, since more and more organizations are evolving knowledge-based strategies.

The other strategic focus that shows high correlations with HR strategy is organizational performance. This finding is confirmation of the relationship between human capital management and most organizational improvement approaches. Apparently organizations recognize that if they want to improve their organizational performance, they need to focus on HR strategy.

All of the HR strategy items show significant correlations with at least two of the strategic focuses. This finding suggests that all are potentially useful activities in at least some organizations. Making rigorous data-based decisions about human capital management is the most broadly related to the business strategic focuses, as it is significantly correlated with all of them.

Partnering with management in developing business strategy and driving change management are both significantly correlated with five of the six focuses. These results are not surprising given that partnering with management and driving change management are ways to be sure that the human capital strategy is aligned with the evolving business strategy.

Conclusion

Overall, the data suggest that HR still has a considerable way to go when it comes to adding value as a strategic player. In most organizations, HR is still not a full partner in the strategy process. On the encouraging side, the HR executives do report being active in a number of areas that are directly tied to the strategic direction of the business. These range all the way from human capital recruitment and development through organization design and strategy development. The challenge for HR is to increase the degree to which it is involved in strategy-related activities, so that it can become a full partner in the high value-added area of business strategy.

CHAPTER 5

HR Decision Science

The growing recognition that human capital decisions must become more sophisticated and strategically relevant represents a challenge for both HR managers and other managers. Consistent with the tenets of decision science in other fields, the key issues involve not only the overall sophistication and quality of human capital decisions, but also the quality of the principles underlying those decisions. High-quality decisions can occur only if HR executives and other managers and employees understand how human capital affects organizational effectiveness and sustainable success, and if they use that understanding to make key human capital allocation decisions. To date, there has been no systematic research on the decision science that is used by HR and other business leaders when they make human capital decisions.

The Quality of Decisions About Talent and Human Capital

Table 5.1 compares the responses of HR executives to those of other managers on questions designed to tap the state of the decision science for HR management. It shows that managers outside of HR perceive significantly greater business leader decision quality than do HR executives. Table 5.1 shows this is true for the first question that taps the general definition of Talentship: "decisions that depend upon or impact human capital are as rigorous, logical and strategically relevant as decisions about more tangible resources." It is also true for business leaders' use of sound principles in four of the six areas of behavioral science. When it comes to the use of sound principles in "development and learning," "labor markets," "culture," and "organization design," managers outside of HR rate themselves significantly higher than HR managers rate them. Both HR executives and managers give business leaders higher marks for using sound principles of business strategy than they do for decision-making principles reflecting organizational behavior issues ranging from motivation to organization design.

HR executives and managers perceive HR leaders as providing unique strategic insights equally, and to a moderate extent. The last two items in Table 5.1 refer to "talent segmentation," understanding where and why human capital makes the biggest difference in their business (Boudreau & Ramstad, 2005c). Managers rate both HR leaders and business leaders higher than HR executives rate them. Interestingly, both HR leaders and managers outside of HR rate HR leaders slightly higher on this capability.

Overall, high-quality decisions and sound decision principles are per-

Table 5.1. HR Decision-making

Decision-making	HR Executives		Managers	
	Mean	Correlation with HR Role in Strategy	Mean	Correlation with HR Role in Strategy
Business leaders' decisions that depend upon or affect human capital (e.g. layoffs, rewards, etc.) are as rigorous, logical, and strategically relevant as their decisions about resources such as money, technology, and customers.	3.1	.40***	3.5[1]	.23*
Business leaders understand and use sound principles when making decisions about:				
1. Motivation	2.9	.50***	3.1	.16
2. Development and learning	2.9	.46***	3.3[1]	.18
3. Labor markets	2.9	.34***	3.2[1]	.28*
4. Culture	3.1	.40***	3.4[1]	.07
5. Organizational design	3.0	.41***	3.3[1]	.17
6. Business strategy	3.7	.44***	3.5	.15
HR leaders identify unique strategy insights by connecting human capital issues to business strategy.	3.1	.44***	3.1	.47***
HR leaders have a good understanding about where and why human capital makes the biggest difference in their business.	3.3	.38***	3.6[1]	.29*
Business leaders have a good understanding about where and why human capital makes the biggest difference in their business.	3.0	.31**	3.4[1]	.16

Scale response: 1 = little or no extent; 2 = some extent; 3 = moderate extent; 4 = great extent; 5 = very great extent.

[1] Significant difference ($p \leq 0.05$) between HR executives and managers in 2004.

Significance level: [t] $p \leq 0.10$ * $p \leq 0.05$ ** $p \leq 0.01$ *** $p \leq 0.001$

ceived as only moderately likely to exist. Managers generally perceive them to exist to a greater extent than HR executives, particularly when they are rating their own capabilities. Either HR executives significantly underestimate the sophistication of their counterparts, or managers overestimate their sophistication. While we cannot resolve this question with these data, our experience suggests that it is a bit of both.

On the one hand, managers have undoubtedly increased their awareness of the importance of human capital, and of their role in nurturing and deploying it. HR data and scorecards are more readily available, providing a basis for improved decisions (see Chapter 11).

On the other hand, there is a great deal that managers still do not know about principles such as talent segmentation, motivation, culture, and learning. HR executives can likely see this gap, and it is reflected in their ratings. HR managers often say "our business leaders don't know what they don't know" when it comes to sound principles of human capital decisions. It is easy for managers to regard their performance as sufficient, while those familiar with the science of human resource management more readily see that much more could be accomplished.

HR leaders, who see room for improvement that their counterparts may not see, need to provide tangible examples when applying more sophisticated human capital decision principles. Our research and experience suggest that just as with the early development of the decision sciences of marketing and finance, in the immediate future we will see significant developments in the sophistication of HR's decision science. As it develops, it will become clear that competing effectively with and through human capital requires that *both* HR managers and managers in general must not be satisfied with the traditional HR service-delivery paradigm. They must extend it to include making better decisions about human capital where it matters most to strategic success.

HR Decision Science Sophistication and HR's Role in Strategy

Table 5.1 also shows the correlations between the HR decision science questions and the perception of HR's role in strategy. The results differ markedly between HR executives and other managers. The HR executives' pattern suggests that all of the decision science elements are related to HR managers' perceptions of their involvement in business strategy, because every item is very significantly and positively correlated with HR's perceived role in strategy.

The responses of other managers suggest a more particular view. The results for the first item, about whether business leaders' decisions about human capital are of the same quality as decisions about other resources, show that both HR and other managers' ratings relate significantly to HR's role in business strategy, but the correlation for HR managers is much stronger. The six items about sound principles used in decision making all have a pattern in which HR managers' ratings relate strongly to their perceptions of HR's role in strategy, but other managers' ratings do not. Only one item, "labor markets," was statistically significantly correlated with HR's role in strategy for both types of - managers, and again the correlation for the non-HR managers was much weaker.

The questions that focus on HR leaders and whether they generate unique strategic insights and understand talent segmentation show a similar pattern for HR leaders and managers. Both groups' ratings show a strong relationship to HR's perceived role in strategy. Finally, the item focused on business leaders' understanding of talent segmentation reflects the pattern of the HR leader ratings being highly correlated with their perceptions of HR's role in strategy, but for non-HR managers they are not.

Generally, it appears that the capability of HR leaders to use sound human capital decision principles and understand talent segmentation is positively related to HR's role in strategy, by both HR and non-HR managers. However, when it comes to similar capabilities for business leaders, only the ratings of the HR leaders show this relationship. Non-HR manager ratings of their own human capital decision capabilities are not related to their ratings of HR's role in strategy. Managers outside of HR differentiated between HR leaders' and non-HR leaders' capabilities. Managers associate HR's decision science quality with HR's strategic involvement, whereas HR executives associate decision science quality on the part of *both HR leaders and business leaders* with the level of HR strategy involvement.

Perhaps HR executives are much more aware of their role in the strategy process, and thus can better understand the benefits of having business leaders who share some sophistication about the science behind human capital decisions. Managers may be less aware of those benefits, and their responses may reflect a more naïve view that it is only the skill of the HR leaders that is important. It is also possible that managers' perceptions are closer to reality, and that the HR executives' results may overestimate the importance of business leader sophistication.

We do not know the causal direction of the relationships with strategy involvement. Thus, these results might suggest that when organizations achieve high HR strategy involvement, HR executives may perceive themselves and their business leaders as better on all elements of the HR decision science, and managers may perceive HR leaders to be better at talent segmentation and providing unique strategic insights. Thus, the causal direction may go from involvement to decision-science sophistication. This interpretation is consistent with the typical situation that we see in organizations, where only a handful of HR leaders are highly skilled at talent segmentation and strategic insights, and many of them developed that ability through career opportunities to observe and participate in business strategy. This interpretation supports efforts to get HR leaders more involved in strategy, as a way to enhance the HR decision science.

Our results suggest that some HR leaders are already "at the table" and have opportunities for full partnership in strategy development and implementation, but that both HR executives and other managers are not satisfied with HR's capability. When this is the case, the causal direction is more likely to be that enhancing the decision science will enhance HR strategic involvement. In that case our results from both managers and HR executives suggest that HR's strategic involvement can be increased by improving HR leaders' decision science capability and unique human capital strategy insights. The results from HR executives additionally suggest that HR's strategic involvement can be enhanced by improving the human capital decision science of managers. In either case, these results show that HR executives and managers both perceive the quality of HR's decision science to be related to the level of HR's involvement in strategy. There may be great value in achieving a stronger meeting of minds among HR managers and other managers regarding the value and importance of enhancing the sophistication of the HR decision science among business leaders. The data from HR executives suggest that HR's strategic involvement can be enhanced by improving the quality of the human capital decision science among both HR executives and business leaders.

Strategic Focuses

Table 5.2 shows the relationship between decision making and strategic focuses. It reports the correlations between the extent to which organizations are pursuing different strategic focuses and the extent to which they perceive the different elements of a sophisticated HR decision science, as reported by HR executives. Clearly, the pattern of significant correlations varies greatly with different strategic focuses.

The extent to which HR decisions by business leaders are made with the same rigor as decisions about other key resources is strongly related to an emphasis on growth and on organizational performance, but not to the other strategic focuses. This finding may reflect the fact that in these two areas there is a relatively greater need to create synergies between human capital resources and the other key resources of the organization. An emphasis on the core business, on quality/speed, or on information-based strategies may motivate a strong focus on specific resources such as money, technology, or marketing. In such situations, business leaders may or may not also be adept at decisions about human capital, but it may be less critical to gaining a competitive advantage.

It is interesting that there is not a strong correlation between the emphasis on knowledge-based strategies and the relative sophistication of business leaders' human capital decisions. However, there are strong and significant positive correlations between the knowledge-based emphasis and business leaders' sophistication about underlying HR decision science principles. The emphasis on knowledge-based strategy also has some of the strongest positive associations with the sophistication of HR's strategic insights and talent segmentation, as well as with business leaders' understanding of talent segmentation. Organizations

Table 5.2. Relationship of HR Decision-making to Strategic Focuses

Decision-making	Strategic Focuses					
	Growth	Core Business	Quality and Speed	Information-Based Strategies	Knowledge-Based Strategies	Organizational Performance
Business leaders' decisions that depend upon or affect human capital (e.g., layoffs, rewards, etc.) are as rigorous, logical, and strategically relevant as their decisions about resources such as money, technology, and customers.	.32**	-.01	.05	.08	.05	.25*
Business leaders understand and use sound principles when making decisions about						
1. Motivation	.27**	.02	.09	.15	.25*	.41***
2. Development and learning	.31**	.11	.17^t	.12	.26**	.30**
3. Labor markets	.38***	.15	.27**	.25*	.40***	.29**
4. Culture	.33***	.08	.21*	.23*	.29**	.25*
5. Organizational design	.33***	.06	.31**	.16	.23*	.22*
6. Business strategy	.33***	.03	.15	.08	.26**	.24*
HR leaders identify unique strategy insights by connecting human capital issues to business strategy.	.22*	.12	.19^t	.16	.31**	.12
HR leaders have a good understanding about where and why human capital makes the biggest difference in their business.	.13	.07	.17^t	.01	.23*	.09
Business leaders have a good understanding about where and why human capital makes the biggest difference in their business.	.22*	.09	.14	.11	.27**	.18^t

Significance level: $^t p \leq 0.10$ $^* p \leq 0.05$ $^{**} p \leq 0.01$ $^{***} p \leq 0.001$

that emphasize knowledge-based strategies may have business leaders who rely on HR leaders to make key human capital decisions. However, their business leaders are expected to bring a high level of sophistication to the decision process, in partnership with sophisticated strategic HR leaders who drive the ultimate decisions.

The six questions that focus on the specific principles underlying business leader decision science sophistication, and the last item in Table 5.2 that focuses on business leader understanding of talent segmentation, present a consistent pattern. They are all strongly associated with the focus on growth, knowledge-based strategies, and performance. These strategic focuses often rely on integrating human capital with other resources. Thus, it may be important that business leaders have a good knowledge of human capital decision principles relative to information-based and quality/speed-based strategies that may focus more on one specific resource or outcome.

The focus on an organization's performance shows strong relationships with all of the elements of business-leader decision science sophistication, but has no significant relationship with either of the HR decision science items. This finding may reflect a tendency for those who emphasize organizational performance to streamline staff functions by pushing greater decision responsibility and decision-science sophistication on business leaders, and to other improvement-oriented groups, such as six-sigma functions, that carry out performance improvement initiatives for the line. Thus, not only is there not a division of labor with HR, but in fact the decision science may rest completely in the hands of business leaders. The extent to which firms report they are pursuing a core business strategy does not appear to be associated strongly with HR decision science sophistication. Those who strongly pursue this strategy are no more or less likely to have sophisticated human capital decision capabilities than those who do not pursue it. It may be that when organizations focus on the core business, they can compete effectively without a highly developed HR decision science, because this focus implies little change and simplifies the organizational and competitive environment. Thus, there is no particular tendency to develop the HR decision science among either HR or business leaders.

The emphasis on information-based strategies is positively correlated with perceptions of business leader sophistication only regarding principles of labor markets and culture. This finding is in sharp contrast to the results for knowledge-based strategies, which show significant correlations for the items about business-leader sophistication on all of the human capital principles. It may be that information-based strategies focus most on quickly acquiring and keeping the right technologies and technical talent, and thus emphasize business leader roles in labor markets and culture, leaving other areas to HR.

There appear to be some nuances about the division of labor between HR and business leaders. The focus on growth and knowledge-based strategies, and to a somewhat lesser degree, quality/speed, seems to be associated with both HR and business leader sophistication. Strategies based on organizational performance seem to be associated with sophistication among business leaders but not HR executives. Information-based and core business strategies show much less association with any of the elements of human capital decision-science sophistication.

The results as they concern the sophistication of HR leaders' strategic human capital insights and talent segmentation are interesting. As might be expected, for growth and knowledge-based strategies, there is a strong relationship to HR's unique strategic insights and/or HR's talent segmentation capability. This is also true, to a lesser degree, for the emphasis on quality and speed.

The sophistication of the human capital decision science appears to relate very differently to different strategic focuses. There is little doubt that a more sophisticated decision science among business leaders and/or HR leaders seems to be associated with many of the strategic emphases we examined. In fact, fieldwork by Boudreau and Ramstad suggests that organizational change results when both HR and business leaders increase the sophistication of their human capital decision science. This is particularly true when they do it collaboratively and while developing a common language and framework for such decisions. Thus, it may be that organizations pursuing growth, knowledge-based, or quality/speed strategies are further along the learning curve, having discovered the value of synergies between business leader and HR decision science sophistication.

Conclusion

HR executives and managers rate human capital decision making as moderately effective. Thus, there is significant room for improvement. That said, business leaders rate the development and quality of the decision making significantly more positively than do their HR counterparts. We suspect this rating is a combination of HR managers' tendency to be self-critical about their strategic contribution and a very real lack of understanding among managers of the richness and analytical value of principles of labor markets, human capital, industrial psychology, and other disciplines. As non-HR managers begin to appreciate the emerging decision science, we suspect their standards of excellence will rise.

HR executives and managers also view the relationship between the sophistication of human capital decision science and HR's strategic involvement differently. HR managers display a very significant association between all elements of the decision science and HR's perceived strategic involvement, whereas managers see almost no relationship. Again, we suspect that this is a case in which managers may not yet "know what they don't know," and that as the language, frameworks, and shared mindsets evolve we will see increasing recognition that the quality of decision science is related to the quality of HR involvement in strategy.

The relationship with different strategy focuses suggests that organizations with different strategic imperatives may create different "divisions of labor" with regard to the human capital decision science. Some organizations seem to build sophistication in both HR and business leaders, while others seem to build it only among HR leaders, and still others only among non-HR leaders. It will be interesting to see if over time there is a convergence toward a shared approach, or if the division of labor persists.

Creating a Strategic Human Resources Organization

CHAPTER 6

HR Organizational Design

A series of questions in our survey examined the extent to which various organizational and operational approaches are employed by HR functions. These approaches were chosen because they may facilitate HR's becoming more of a business partner and, in some cases, a strategic partner. The approaches factored into five scales. The scales and the mean responses to the items are shown in Table 6.1.

Current Design

The practices used the most are those concerned with decentralization, service teams, and resource efficiency approaches. A particularly popular practice from 1995 to 2004 is to have decentralized generalists who support a business unit. This configuration is a possible way to position HR as a business partner. A comparison of the 1995 and 2004 results shows there has been a significant increase in the use of HR service teams and centers of excellence. These same approaches show significant differences when 1995 is compared to 2001.

The greater use of corporate centers of excellence complements the use of decentralized generalists by giving them a source of expert help. Growth in the use of HR service teams is consistent with findings from other studies showing that teams are an increasingly popular way to combine the talents and knowledge of various contributors to deliver integrated services.

There is a significant *decrease* in the degree to which HR practices vary across business units. This finding suggests that while there may be dedicated HR leaders supporting businesses, their role is not to tailor HR practices to those businesses but rather to work with centers of excellence and HR service teams in order to deliver common services to their parts of the organization.

The use of common practices most likely reflects efforts to simplify and to achieve scale leverage in some HR activities, and the tendency of companies to be in fewer diverse businesses. There are economies of scale to be gained when corporations use the same HR practices in all their units. This is particularly true in the case of transactions and the creation of IT-based self-service HR activities.

The relatively strong focus on resource efficiency is not surprising, given the cost challenges that most organizations faced in 2004. The most popular approaches to controlling costs include sharing services,

Table 6.1. HR Organization — Current

HR Organization	1995	1998	2001	2004	Correlation with HR Role in Strategy
HR Service Teams	**2.9**	**3.3**	**3.3**	**3.5**[1]	**.36*****
Centers of excellence provide specialized expertise.	2.5	3.1	3.1	3.3[1]	.27**
HR teams provide service and support the business.	2.9	3.4	3.5	3.8[1]	.27**
HR systems and policies are developed through joint line/HR task teams.	3.3	3.3	3.2	3.3	.19[t]
Decentralization	**3.2**	**3.1**	**3.2**	**3.0**	**-.08**
Decentralized HR generalists support business units.	3.6	3.9	4.0	3.9	-.00
HR practices vary across business units.	2.9	2.6	2.6	2.3[1]	-.28**
Very small corporate staff — most HR managers and professionals are out in businesses.	2.9	2.8	3.0	2.8	.09
Resource Efficiency	—	—	—	**3.0**	**.24***
Administrative processing is centralized in shared services units.	3.5	3.4	3.4	3.7	.07
Self-funding requirements exist for HR services.	1.7	1.9	1.9	2.1[1]	.08
Low HR/employee ratio	—	—	—	3.1	.20[t]
Low cost of HR services	—	—	—	3.2	.18[t]
Information Technology	—	—	—	**2.7**	**.25***
Transactional work is outsourced.	—	2.3	2.3	2.5	.10
Some activities that used to be done by HR are now done by line managers.	2.6	2.6	2.6	2.8	.19[t]
Some transactional activities that used to be done by HR are done by employees on a self-service basis.	—	2.3	2.5	2.9	.17[t]
Efficient and accurate HRIS	—	—	—	3.3	.24*
Data automatically gathered for tracking effectiveness of HR programs	—	—	—	2.3	.20*
HR "advice" is available on-line for managers and employees	—	—	—	2.5	.18[t]
HR Talent Development	—	—	—	**2.4**	**.26***
People rotate within HR.	2.6	2.8	2.8	2.8	.18[t]
People rotate into HR.	1.8	1.8	1.8	1.8	.20[t]
People rotate out of HR to other functions.	1.8	1.9	1.9	1.9	.15
Hire from the outside for senior HR positions	—	—	—	2.9	.08

Means; response scale: 1 = little or not extent, 2 = some extent, 3 = moderate extent, 4 = great extent, 5 = very great extent

[1] Significant difference ($p \le .05$) between 1995 and 2004.

Significance level: [t] $p \le 0.10$ * $p \le 0.05$ ** $p \le 0.01$ *** $p \le 0.001$

Table 6.2. Relationship of Strategic Focuses — Current Organization

HR Organization	Growth	Core Business	Quality and Speed	Information-Based Strategies	Knowledge-Based Strategies	Organizational Performance
				Strategic Focuses		
HR service teams	.21*	.38***	.27**	.20*	.35***	.30**
Decentralization	.14	.09	-.23*	-.22*	.07	-.08
Resource efficiency	.08	.17^t	-.04	.09	.06	.22*
Information technology	.22*	.38***	.10	.17^t	.20*	.24*
HR talent development	.03	.21*	.17^t	.17^t	.37***	.24*

Significance level: ^{t} $p \leq 0.10$ * $p \leq 0.05$ ** $p \leq 0.01$ *** $p \leq 0.001$

transferring tasks to line managers, self-service approaches, and having a low HR/employee ratio.

The practices used the least are self-funding of HR services and employee rotation into and out of HR. The lack of rotation is potentially a major problem for the HR function because it means that its members are likely to remain a separate group with a unique perspective, and not be involved in or deeply knowledgeable about the business. There also appears to be relatively little rotation within HR, a practice that creates silo careers and does little to help HR employees develop an understanding of the total HR function.

There are a number of significant relationships between the way that HR is organized and managed and the role it plays in strategy. Of the five areas, only decentralization is not significantly related to HR's role in strategy. Having HR practices that vary across business units is significantly negatively related to HR's role in strategy. Overall, decentralization is slightly, although not significantly, negatively related to HR's role in strategy. In many ways this is understandable. Decentralization can lead to a lack of corporate presence and limit the opportunity for HR to play a major role in corporate strategy decisions.

HR talent development, information technology, resource efficiency, and HR service teams are all significantly related to HR's role in strategy. In order to be a strategic partner, HR needs to use information technology, have good talent, perform its own operations effectively, and have expertise and services that meet the needs of the business.

Table 6.2 shows the relationships between the strategic focuses and HR organizational approaches. The use of service teams is significantly associated with all of the strategic focuses, indicating the importance of bringing multiple sources of knowledge to bear on strategy implementation. HR talent development and information technology are also associated with multiple strategic focuses. Resource efficiency and decentralization have minimal relationships to the business's strategic focuses.

Several of the organizational strategic focuses are significantly associated with multiple HR organization initiatives. Core business, knowledge-based, and organizational performance strategies all show relationships to the use of teams, HR IT, and HR talent development. The significant negative relationship between both quality and speed and information-based strategies with decentralization may reflect a strong emphasis on centralizing HR to improve cost and efficiency (in the case of quality strategies) and information standardization and sharing (in the case of information-based strategies).

Future Design

For the first time, in the 2004 survey, HR executives were asked to indicate how they see the HR function operating in the future. Table 6.3 presents the results, which suggest some important shifts in the future. Service teams and information technology received the highest ratings, 2.5 and 2.6 on a 3-point scale, indicating that these are viewed as likely and important focuses for the future. The highest ratings for individual items went to two of the items involving information technology. It is very clear that organizations intend to use HR technology to enable employees to serve themselves. This, of course, is only possible if the organization has an efficient and accurate HR information system (HRIS), clearly another top priority for these organizations.

The results also suggest that organizations will make greater use of centers of excellence, service teams, shared service units, and decentralized generalists to support the business units. At the same time, there is a notably low rating for HR practices that vary across business units and for self-funding of HR practices, suggesting that companies will continue to look for advantages of scale.

There is little evidence that organizations intend to do a great deal more with respect to rotation in the HR function. Apparently, this idea simply has not caught on, despite the fact that it has the potential to support the career development of HR employees.

Plans to shift toward the greater use of service teams and a greater emphasis on HR talent development are both associated with HR's having a more strategic role. Future plans in the other three areas of HR organization shown in Table 6.3 are not significantly related to HR's role in strategy. A significant relationship with HR talent development proba-

Table 6.3. HR Organization — Future

HR Organization	Mean	Correlation with HR Role in Strategy
HR Service Teams	**2.5**	**.27****
Centers of excellence provide specialized expertise.	2.6	.25*
HR teams provide service and support the business.	2.6	.15
HR systems and policies are developed through joint line/HR task teams.	2.4	.12
Decentralization	**2.1**	**.08**
Decentralized HR generalists support business units.	2.5	.07
HR practices vary across business units.	1.7	-.14
Very small corporate staff — most HR managers and professionals are out in businesses.	2.1	.16
Resource Efficiency	**2.2**	**.17**
Administrative processing is centralized in shared services units.	2.6	.06
Self-funding requirements exist for HR services.	1.7	.03
Low HR/employee ratio.	2.2	.07
Low cost of HR services.	2.4	.20^t
Information Technology	**2.6**	**.09**
Transactional work is outsourced.	2.2	.01
Some activities that used to be done by HR are now done by line managers.	2.5	.09
Some transactional activities that used to be done by HR are done by employees on a self-service basis.	2.8	-.03
Efficient and accurate HRIS.	2.9	-.04
Data automatically gathered for tracking effectiveness of HR Programs.	2.5	.19^t
HR "advice" is available on-line for managers and employees.	2.4	.03
HR Talent Development	**2.0**	**.31****
People rotate within HR.	2.3	.26*
People rotate into HR.	1.9	.28**
People rotate out of HR to other functions.	1.9	.26*
Hire from the outside for senior HR positions	1.9	.02

Means; response scale: 1 = not in our plans, 2 = possible focus, 3 = an important future focus

Significance level: ^{t} $p \leq 0.10$ * $p \leq 0.05$ ** $p \leq 0.01$ *** $p \leq 0.001$

Table 6.4. Relationship of Strategic Focuses — Future Organization

HR Organization	Strategic Focuses					
	Growth	Core Business	Quality and Speed	Information-Based Strategies	Knowledge-Based Strategies	Organizational Performance
HR service teams	-.04	.24*	.10	.08	.20^t	.01
Decentralization	.06	.23*	-.06	-.22*	.17	-.02
Resource efficiency	.01	.21*	.16	.11	.28**	.23*
Information technology	-.03	.19^t	.08	.07	.25*	-.01
HR talent development	.02	.20^t	.01	.12	.25*	.08

Significance level:　　　$^t p \leq 0.10$　　　$^* p \leq 0.05$　　　$^{**} p \leq 0.01$　　　$^{***} p \leq 0.001$

bly indicates that when HR is involved in strategy, it recognizes the importance of developing people with both a broad understanding of HR and an understanding of the business. The expected growth in the use of such things as centers of excellence most likely reflects the importance of having corporate expertise that can interface with the strategy development process.

Table 6.4 shows the relationships between the strategic focuses and the future of the HR organization. The relationships that particularly stand out are those having to do with knowledge-based strategies. When an organization has a knowledge-based strategy, it is more likely to plan to use most of the HR organization approaches that were studied, with the exception of decentralization. There is an interesting contrast with regard to decentralization. Those companies pursuing a core business strategy are significantly more likely to decentralize HR, whereas those pursuing an information-based strategy are significantly less likely to decentralize it. This finding may reflect the desire to make full use of centralized information-based systems by centralizing HR, whereas in core business organizations it may reflect a desire to give businesses maximum flexibility in shaping HR to fit their individual strategies.

Conclusion

Overall, the results show relatively little change in the utilization of various HR organizational approaches from 1995 to 2004. There has been significant growth in service teams and centers of excellence, changes that are related to HR's being more of a strategic partner. But we did not see greater adoption of such things as the career movement of individuals or joint line/HR task teams. There seems to be a trend toward less emphasis on HR practices that vary across business units and on self-service HR practices.

The results do strongly suggest that an organization's strategy has significant effects on the HR organization. The HR organization's design is significantly associated with strategies that focus on core business and knowledge management. However, the degree to which organizations pursue other strategies is less systematically related to the use of various HR organization design features. This may reflect the fact that it is less apparent which HR organizational design features contribute to those strategies in general, or that a variety of HR organization approaches may work equally well.

CHAPTER 7

*Human Resources
Activities*

To get an in-depth sense of the changes that are occurring in the role of HR, we asked whether the focus on a number of human resources activities has increased, stayed the same, or decreased over the past five to seven years. Data analyses showed six clusters of human resources activities, with two activity items (HRIS and unions) that did not cluster with any others. Table 7.1 shows these activities and how companies responded in 1995, 1998, 2001, and 2004.

HR Activity Levels

Our respondents reported the largest increases in level of activity in the areas of organizational design and development, recruitment and selection, compensation and benefits, employee development, and human resources information systems (just as was true in 1995, 1998, and 2001). They reported not increasing their organization's focus in just two areas, union relations and record keeping (both of these activities were rated at "stayed the same" in the 2004 results). As HR functions take on new responsibilities, they do not seem to be decreasing their focus on the old ones.

A comparison of the 1995, 1998, 2001, and 2004 data shows some significant differences in the amount of increase reported. The largest increase from 1995 is in recruitment and selection, a result that may have been initially driven by the war for talent that occurred during the 1990s. Even though that era is over, and there is much talk of being in a period of "jobless growth," the focus on recruitment and selection continues to increase, perhaps reflecting a growing recognition of the importance of human capital.

A comparison of the 2001 and the 2004 results shows that the largest increase in focus was on benefits. This increase most likely reflects the rising costs of health care and retirement benefits as well as the growth in flexible benefit plans.

Table 7.1 also shows the correlations between the changes in focus on human resource activities and HR's role in strategy. Not surprisingly, the highest single correlation is between organization design and development activities and HR's role in strategy. Strategic change often is closely associated with the need to develop new capabilities and designs. A related finding is the strong relationship between growth in attention to employee development and HR's strategic role This finding follows logically from the need to change the employee skill set when

Table 7.1. Change in Focus on HR Activities During Past Five to Seven Years

HR Activities	1995	1998	2001	2004	Correlation with HR Role in Strategy
Design and Organizational Development	—	**3.8**	**3.9**	**3.9**	**.37*****
HR planning	4.1	3.9	4.0	4.1	.12
Organizational development	4.0	3.8	3.9	3.8	.25*
Organizational design	—	3.6	3.7	3.6	.32***
Strategic planning	—	3.8	3.8	4.0	.43***
Compensation and Benefits	**3.9**	**3.7**	**3.8**	**4.0**	**.00**
Compensation	3.9	3.8	3.9	3.9	.02
Benefits	3.9	3.6	3.6	4.0	-.02
Legal and Regulatory	—	**3.1**	**3.1**	**3.1**	**-.05**
Employee record keeping	2.8	2.8	2.7	3.0	-.11
Legal affairs	3.4	3.3	3.3	3.3	-.03
Affirmative action	3.3	3.1	3.1	3.2	.03
Employee assistance	—	3.1	3.2	3.1	-.01
Employee Development	—	—	3.6	**3.8**	**.32*****
Employee training/education	3.8	3.5	3.7	3.7	.30**
Management development	3.9	3.8	3.8	4.0	.30**
Performance appraisal	3.8	3.5	3.7	3.9	.17^ت
Career planning	3.3	3.4	3.3	3.3	.18^t
Competency / talent assessment	—		3.7	3.8	.25*
Recruitment and Selection	3.4	3.9	3.8	**3.8**[1]	**.18^t**
Recruitment	3.3	3.9	3.8	3.8[1]	.20^t
Selection	3.5	3.8	3.7	3.8[1]	.14
Metrics	—	—	—	**3.7**	**.24***
Data analysis and mining	—	—	—	3.6	.21*
HR metrics	—	—	—	3.8	.23*
HR Information Systems	4.1	4.1	4.0	4.0	-.14
Union	3.1	2.9	2.7	3.0	.01

Means; scale response: 1 = decreased, 3 = stayed the same, 5 = increased.

[1] Significant difference ($p \le .05$) between 1995 and 2004.

Significance level: ^{t} $p \le 0.10$ * $p \le 0.05$ ** $p \le 0.01$ *** $p \le 0.001$

Table 7.2. Relationship of Strategic Focuses to HR Activities

HR Activities	Strategic Focuses					
	Growth	Core Business	Quality and Speed	Information-Based Strategies	Knowledge-Based Strategies	Organizational Performance
Design and organizational development	.05	.04	.33***	.38***	.40***	.25*
Compensation and benefits	-.03	-.03	.31**	.11	.13	.10
Legal and regulatory	-.06	-.06	-.03	.11	.21*	.10
Employee development	.19^t	-.04	.22*	.17^t	.36***	.18^t
Recruitment and selection	-.03	-.01	.20*	.25*	.26**	.15
Metrics	.08	.08	-.01	.17^t	.30**	.24*
HRIS	.05	.05	.07	.13	.04	.00
Union relations	-.01	.16	-.08	-.03	-.04	-.01

Significance level: ^{t} $p \leq 0.10$ * $p \leq 0.05$ ** $p \leq 0.01$ *** $p \leq 0.001$

organizational capabilities and competencies are developed and implemented as part of new strategies. It is interesting that this correlation is higher than the one with respect to recruitment and selection. Apparently, the amount of effort HR spends on developing people is associated more with their strategic role than is the amount of effort spent on recruitment and selection.

The questions on HR metrics and analytics, which were new in 2004, proved enlightening. More focus on metrics and analytics is significantly correlated to HR's role in strategy. Again, this finding is not surprising, since metrics and analytics can be key inputs to both the development of strategy and the successful assessment of strategy implementation. They also often provide a signal of rigor to leaders outside of HR, one that may result in more involvement in strategy and business processes.

Activities and Focuses

Table 7.2 shows the relationships between HR activities and the six strategic focuses. There are some significant relationships here. Strategies that focus on quality and speed relate to an increased focus on design and organizational development, compensation, employee development, and recruitment and selection. This finding is not surprising, since quality and speed are affected by cross-functional process issues that can be addressed through new designs, skill development, and increased organizational alignment.

Creating a Strategic Human Resources Organization

Results for the final three strategic focuses shown in Table 7.2 are very similar. Information, knowledge, and organizational performance strategies all are strongly related to organizational design and development activities. In addition, the more an organization focuses on these three strategic initiatives, the more HR activities are said to increase in employee development, recruitment and selection, and metrics. The most logical explanation for this is that these HR activities focus on key aspects of an organization's performance capability. In order to execute any of the three strategic focuses, an organization needs to build its human capital and its ability to organize human capital. Thus, successful efforts that focus on these strategies require increased attention to organizational design and human capital.

It is somewhat surprising that the growth initiative is not strongly related to an increase in any HR activities. Growth, in particular, creates a number of challenges for HR and might be expected to be at least related to recruitment and selection. It is only weakly related to employee development, which may reflect the need to develop competencies, particularly management and leadership skills, more quickly in a growing organization. With that exception, a growth strategy and a core-business strategy are similar in that they are not related to HR's activities. Apparently, these two business strategies do not entail the kinds of changes that create the need for new HR activities.

Conclusion

Overall, the results do show changes in the focus of HR as well as a relationship between those changes and the strategic direction of the business. Particularly interesting is the increased focus on design and organizational development when the strategic focuses of quality/speed, information, knowledge, and organization performance are present. Organization design and development is an area that has not always been a focus of HR. It is, however, an area that is closely tied to organizational performance and business strategy. Providing expertise in this area appears to be a way for HR to become more of a business partner. Organizations with strategic focuses on knowledge, information, and organizational performance tend to have an increased focus on HR activities that involve human capital management, organization design, and metrics.

CHAPTER 8

Outsourcing

Outsourcing is a potential way to improve the effectiveness of the HR function and make it more strategic. In addition to acquiring the expertise of skilled HR professionals, outsourcing can reduce the transactional work of HR organizations and can be a cost reduction method (Lawler, Ulrich, Fitz-enz, and Madden, 2004).

In the best-case scenario, outsourcing companies can provide better and cheaper services because they are focused on a particular process or area of expertise that is their core competency. In addition, they can capture economies of scale by serving multiple organizations. They also can improve the processes of organizations because of the knowledge they possess. At the very least, outsourcing can reduce the number of employees on the HR department payroll and create a flexible cost structure when services are needed occasionally or for short periods of time.

Use of Outsourcing

Table 8.1 shows the degree to which twenty-one HR activities are currently being outsourced. The two items on metrics were asked for the first time in 2004. Activities are grouped by the six factors that our statistical analysis produced; seven items did not group. In 1995, 1998, 2001, and 2004 the use of outsourcing varied widely among the thirty-one activities, but in no case were any of these activities even close to being completely outsourced by all the companies.

In over 90 percent of the companies, HR planning, strategic planning, and performance appraisal were not outsourced at all. Organization design was not outsourced in 89 percent of the companies. These are all areas in which HR can add considerable strategic value and act as a strategic partner. However, as was noted earlier, they are not all areas in which HR is particularly active (e.g., strategic planning and organizational design). They clearly represent areas of opportunity, given their importance.

The most likely area to be completely outsourced was employee assistance, with 59 percent of the companies completely outsourcing it. This finding is hardly surprising, given its personal and confidential nature. Benefits were the next most likely to be partially outsourced, with 77 percent of the companies partially outsourcing it. The frequency of outsourcing of benefits probably reflects the combination of transactional and specialized knowledge work that it involves. In over 50 percent of

Table 8.1. Outsourcing Use

Type of Outsourcing	Percentages			Mean				Correlation with HR Role in Strategy
	Not at All	Partially	Completely	1995	1998	2001	**2004**	
Overall Outsourcing				—	—	1.4	**1.3**	**.09**
Planning				—	1.1	1.1	**1.1**	**-.02**
HR planning	96	4	0	1.0	1.1	1.0	1.0	-.20*
Strategic planning	93	7	0	—	1.1	1.1	1.1	.13
Organizational Design/ Development				—	1.2	1.2	**1.2**	**-.07**
Organizational development	78	22	0	1.3	1.3	1.2	1.2	-.09
Organizational design	89	12	0	—	1.2	1.1	1.1	-.02
Training				1.6	1.7	1.7	**1.7**	**-.02**
Employee training/education	24	76	0	1.6	1.9	1.8	1.8	.08
Management development	45	54	1	1.5	1.6	1.6	1.6	-.08
HRIS and Record Keeping				1.2	1.5	1.4	**1.5[1]**	**.13**
HR information systems	55	40	4	1.3	1.6	1.5	1.5	.08
Employee record keeping	59	33	7	1.2	1.4	1.3	1.5[1]	.14
Staffing and Career Development				1.2	1.2	1.2	**1.3[1]**	**.12**
Performance appraisal	91	8	1	1.0	1.1	1.1	1.1[1]	.07
Recruitment	43	56	1	1.4	1.6	1.5	1.6[1]	.01
Selection	76	24	0	1.2	1.2	1.2	1.2	.13
Career planning	88	13	0	1.1	1.2	1.2	1.1	.09
Metrics				—	—	—	**1.2**	**.19[t]**
Data analysis and mining	82	16	2	—	—	—	1.2	.11
HR metrics	87	12	2	—	—	—	1.2	.22*
Benefits	11	77	12	1.7	1.9	1.9	**2.0[1]**	**-.12**
Compensation	60	40	0	1.2	1.5	1.5	**1.4[1]**	**.09**
Legal Affairs	43	52	5	1.4	1.6	1.6	**1.6[1]**	**.16**
Affirmative Action	67	26	6	1.1	1.2	1.3	**1.4[1]**	**-.02**
Employee Assistance	12	29	59	—	2.2	2.3	**2.5**	**.10**
Competency / Talent Assessment	57	38	5	—	—	1.3	**1.5**	**.21***
Union Relations	86	13	1	1.1	1.1	1.1	**1.2**	**.05**

Significance level: [t] $p \leq 0.10$ * $p \leq 0.05$ ** $p \leq 0.01$ *** $p \leq 0.001$

[1] Significant difference ($p \leq .05$) between 1995 and 2004.

the companies, training, recruitment, and legal affairs were partially or completely outsourced.

Overall, the use of outsourcing occurs in areas where specialized expertise is involved, such as legal affairs, and areas where primarily transactional work occurs, such as benefits administration. This result provides confirmation that organizations are outsourcing to gain both transactional efficiency and expertise.

A comparison between the 1995 and 2004 results shows a general, although small, increase in the use of outsourcing. Specifically, there were statistically significant increases in the use of outsourcing from 1995 to 2004 in the following areas: record keeping, compensation, recruitment, performance appraisal, affirmative action, and legal affairs. Only organizational development was less likely to be outsourced in 2004 than it was in 1995, and the difference is not significant.

The comparison among the 1998, 2001, and 2004 data shows essentially no change in the frequency of outsourcing. Thus, although outsourcing has increased since 1995, most of that increase essentially took place between 1995 and 1998. Since 1998, our data show little evidence of an increased use of outsourcing; the obvious conclusion at this point is that there is no current trend toward greater use of outsourcing.

Clearly the opportunity exists for more outsourcing to take place, since very few companies completely outsource any of their HR activities and many HR activities are barely outsourced. This finding, of course, raises the question of whether there will be a new wave of outsourcing that will in fact lead to a significant increase in the amount of outsourcing that takes place.

One possibility is that outsourcing will increase because more and more organizations will decide to outsource their HR administration to the growing number of HR business process outsourcing (BPO) firms that exist (Lawler, Ulrich, Fitz-enz, and Madden, 2004). However, there is little reason to believe there will be a significant increase in many of the types of outsourcing that are shown in Table 8.1. In many of these areas, knowledge and understanding of an organization's operations are necessary; as a result, they are much less likely to be outsourced than the kinds of transactional work which are outsourced to HR BPO firms.

Table 8.1 also shows the relationship between outsourcing and the role that HR plays in strategy. In general these two issues are not related. However, a significant correlation does exist between the strategic role of HR and the outsourcing of talent assessment, and a weak relationship between outsourcing of HR metrics and the strategic role of HR. This

Table 8.2. Relationship of Strategic Focuses to Outsourcing

Type of Outsourcing	Strategic Focuses					
	Growth	Core Business	Quality and Speed	Information-Based Strategies	Knowledge-Based Strategies	Organizational Performance
Overall Outsourcing	.11	.14	.02	-.09	.13	.00
Planning	.06	-.02	-.03	-.06	-.05	-.12
Benefits	.11	.10	.10	-.01	.27**	-.04
Organizational design/development	.03	.13	-.01	.09	.13	-.01
Training	.04	.21*	-.07	-.07	.08	-.10
HRIS and record keeping	.12	.06	-.03	-.06	.07	.05
Staffing and career development	.08	-.04	.01	-.09	.02	-.08
Metrics	.03	.09	.03	-.12	.01	.13
Compensation	-.07	.13	-.07	-.19^t	.04	-.07
Legal affairs	-.06	.00	.07	-.03	.03	-.12
Affirmative action	.09	.10	-.04	-.06	-.12	.02
Employee assistance	-.10	.12	.01	-.14	.04	-.10
Competency/talent assessment	-.09	.17	.06	-.08	.02	.08
Union relations	.07	.07	-.05	-.21^t	.02	-.13

Significance level: $^t p \leq 0.10$ $* p \leq 0.05$ $** p \leq 0.01$ $*** p \leq 0.001$

finding may well reflect the fact that HR lacks the internal resources needed to do this work when it becomes a key strategic issue and that, as a result, outsourcing is used. It certainly fits with our earlier finding that these are areas in which activity tends to increase when HR plays a major role in strategy. The question is: will internal HR organizations step up their sophistication in metrics and talent assessment, or will these strategic activities increasingly be done by consultants?

Table 8.2 shows that there are very few significant relationships between strategic focus and outsourcing. In general, this result is not surprising, but the lack of a relationship between growth strategies and outsourcing is surprising, especially given our finding in 1998 that growth-focused organizations were more likely to outsource than other organizations. Growth puts a stress on the human resource delivery capabilities of an organization, and outsourcing could provide a quick way to acquire additional support for an HR function that is under pressure to serve a larger organization. It is not clear why this relationship is not present in either the 2001 or the 2004 data.

Problems with Outsourcing

Table 8.3 presents the responses to a question about the kinds of problems that result from outsourcing. The data suggest that companies have experienced a number of problems in their outsourcing activities, although none of the problems were experienced to a great extent by the majority of the companies.

As was true in 1998 and 2001, in 2004 the most common problems involve the cost and quality of the services delivered. Over 50 percent of the firms said that to a moderate or great extent it is more expensive to administer the outsourcing activity than they had expected and the services are not as good as promised. Over 40 percent say that the switch to alternative outsourcers is difficult, the costs are higher than promised, and that contractors do not have enough knowledge of the company. The picture that emerges is one of companies experiencing problems with outsourcing but finding it difficult to switch to alternative vendors. Particularly disturbing are the reports of poor quality. On the positive side, the number of companies experiencing higher than promised costs decreased from 2001 to 2004.

The problem that occurs the least frequently is the loss of competitive advantage from the way companies manage people. This finding is a bit surprising, since allowing outsourcers to deliver HR services can change the relationship between employees and organizations. It can depersonalize and homogenize it so that organizations lose part of their brand as an employer.

There are at least three explanations for why an organization may not feel it is losing competitive advantage with outsourcing. First, the outsourcing may involve transactional work that is not a key strategic interface with the employees. Second, the organization may have carefully structured its outsourcing arrangements so that its HR programs have unique features that foster the kind of relationship it wants with its employees. Third, many organizations may never have managed their people in a way that gave them a competitive advantage, and thus have little to lose by outsourcing.

Between 2001 and 2004 there were changes in the problems organizations experienced with outsourcing. The biggest decrease has already been mentioned: it has to do with costs being higher than promised. Also decreasing as a concern was contractors' lack of knowledge about the company.

There was a slight increase in the degree to which organizations feel that the switch to the new outsourcer is difficult. It is important not to overinterpret this change because it is only a slight increase, but it may

Table 8.3. Problems in Managing Outsourcing

Problems	Percentages					Mean		
	Little or No Extent	Some Extent	Moderate Extent	Great Extent	Very Great Extent	1998	2001	**2004**
Contractor and Administrative Issues						2.4	2.5	**2.5**
Resources required to manage the contract and relationship have been more than anticipated	21	23	37	14	5	2.5	2.6	**2.6**
Services haven't been as good as promised	18	32	31	14	5	2.7	2.7	**2.6**
Contractors don't know enough about the company	22	34	28	14	2	2.4	2.6	**2.4**
Cost has been higher than promised	30	27	27	14	3	2.5	2.7	**2.3[1]**
Lack of skills for managing contractors	31	31	19	16	3	2.4	2.3	**2.3**
Switch to new outsourcers is very difficult	26	26	28	17	4	2.3	2.3	**2.5**
Effectiveness of Outsourcing						2.0	2.0	**2.0**
Loss of competitive advantage from the way we manage people	64	16	14	4	1	1.6	1.8	**1.6**
Negative reaction from business units served	38	35	15	10	2	2.0	2.0	**2.0**
Negative reaction from company employees	33	34	21	9	2	2.1	2.1	**2.1**
Negative reaction from HR employees	33	37	21	7	2	2.1	2.1	**2.1**
Can't have HR systems we need	40	31	12	12	4	2.1	2.2	**2.1**

[1] Significant difference ($p \leq .05$) between 2001 and 2004.

reflect a growing awareness of the degree to which outsourcing causes a decrease in internal expertise and, therefore, makes it difficult to bring an outsource service back in-house or transfer it to another outsourcer.

Enough concerns about outsourcing were voiced by these companies to raise a caution flag. Before an organization outsources, it needs to develop the capability to manage contractors and must have adequate internal resources to manage them. Costs are also a critical issue; organizations need to pay particular attention to cost control in this area.

Conclusion

Overall, there is little evidence that outsourcing is in a strong growth mode. Organizations may be missing an opportunity, particularly when outsourcing allows them to access knowledge and expertise that they may lack and are not in a good position to develop. They may also be missing a chance to realize economies of scale.

An obstacle to the growth of outsourcing may be the number of problems associated with it, including the apparent difficulty of getting sustained cost and quality advantages. So far, however, none of the problems with outsourcing seem to be increasing in frequency or causing a loss of competitive advantage. Thus there remains a possibility that outsourcing will grow in the future.

Creating a Strategic Human Resources Organization

CHAPTER 9

Use of Information Technology

Information technology (IT) potentially is a powerful way to accomplish HR record keeping, HR transactions, and many other administrative tasks more quickly, efficiently, and accurately, thus enabling HR managers to save money and have more time to spend on strategic business support. IT can be a way to deliver expert advice to managers and employees in areas such as selection, career development, and compensation. It can also facilitate change efforts by assessing the capabilities of the workforce and by providing information and training that supports change. Finally, it can support the development of business strategy by providing important information about the capabilities and core competencies of the organization.

Level of Use

Table 9.1 shows the state of IT-based human resource processes, current and past. In 2004 over 60 percent of companies were using IT for most or all of their human resource systems, a relatively high level of IT use. It represents a significant increase in use from 2001. This increase is not surprising, particularly in light of the great amount of activity occurring in the HR IT world. In many respects, the increase almost had to occur, given the increased popularity of ERP software and the fact that the major ERP vendors have HR applications (e.g., SAP, ORACLE).

Activities

In 1998 we added a series of questions on the use of company-based IT systems to our survey in order to obtain a more complete picture of the capabilities of the systems. We asked about the degree to which employees and managers could do certain HR tasks via an IT system. Table 9.2 shows the results for 1998, 2001, and 2004, grouped on the basis of a statistical factor analysis of the questions.

Perhaps the most striking finding is the variation in the extent to which these HR activities can be carried out by employees and managers with IT systems. Posting job openings, applying for a job (external candidates), personal information changes, and changing benefit coverage are activities that can be done completely by employees or managers in over 60 percent of the companies. At the other extreme, there are six activities, primarily in the area of management tools, that, in 40 percent or more of the companies, cannot be done at all.

What most clearly distinguishes the tasks that are frequently done from

Table 9.1. State of HR Information Technology

State of Technology	Percent			
	1995	**1998**	**2001**	**2004**
Little or no information technology / automation present in the HR function	6.3	8.4	8.3	6.1
Some HR processes are information technology based / automated	45.3	40.3	48.3	32.3
Most processes are information technology based / automated but not fully integrated	40.6	42.9	35.9	48.5
Completely integrated HR information technology / automated system	7.8	8.4	7.6	13.1
Mean	**3.50**	**3.50**	**3.41**	**3.69**

Mean; response scale: 1 = no information technology; 2 = little information technology; 3 = some processes integrated; 4 = most processes integrated; 5 = completely integrated

those that are not is the degree to which the activities are transactional. Transactional activities are particularly likely to be done on an IT system, whereas those involving expert advice and decision-making (e.g., all the management tool items) are either done not at all or done only partially via IT systems.

The difference in use between transactional and advice tools is hardly surprising, since transactions are particularly suited to self-service. It takes much more sophisticated software support to offer advice and training.

More and more companies have invested in IT systems that can help with virtually all the activities in Table 9.2. A comparison between the 2001 and 2004 results shows significant increases in the use of IT for a wide range of activities. A particularly large increase occurred from 1998 to 2004 in the ability to use IT systems for job information. Apparently, organizations have increasingly adopted the Web as a way to handle the entire job application and the job posting processes.

There also is evidence of increased use of IT systems for performance management purposes since 1998. This finding may well reflect the use of IT for 360-degree appraisals and for the general accumulation of performance data throughout an organization. The emergence of standard modules for such data in the major software packages may well be driving this increase.

Creating a Strategic Human Resources Organization

Table 9.2. IT System HR Activities Done by Employees or Managers

Activities	Percentages			Mean			
	Not At All	Partially	Completely	1998	2001	2004	Correlation with HR Role in Strategy
Personnel Records				2.1	2.1	2.5[1]	.18[t]
Change benefit coverage	14	21	65	2.2	2.2	2.5[1]	.08
Change address and/or other personal information	19	18	63	2.0	2.1	2.4[1]	.22*
Job Information				—	2.1	2.4[1]	.18[t]
Apply for a job (external applicants)	9	35	56	1.9	2.2	2.5[1]	.11
Apply for a job (internal applicants)	8	25	67	1.5	2.2	2.6[1]	.15
Post job openings	9	27	64	1.5	2.5	2.5	.28**
Post personal resume/bio	40	31	29	—	1.5	1.9[1]	.04
Employee Training				—	1.7	1.9[1]	**.26***
New hire orientation	39	55	6	—	1.5	1.7[1]	.06
Skills training	19	72	8	—	1.7	1.9[1]	.20*
Scheduling training	21	38	40	—	2.0	2.2[1]	.27**
Management Tools				—	—	1.7	.16
Career development planning	44	49	7	1.4	1.5	1.6[1]	.01
Obtain advice and information on handling personnel issues	40	54	6	1.5	1.5	1.7[1]	.12
Management development training	35	62	3	—	1.5	1.7[1]	.19[t]
Search for employees with specified skills/competencies	47	44	9	—	1.5	1.6	.07
Assess skills/competencies/knowledge	41	49	10	—	—	1.7	.15
Access knowledge communities or experts	55	36	9	—	—	1.5	.11
Access managers tool kit	35	45	20	—	—	1.8	.16
Salary Planning/ Administration	20	47	33	1.9	2.0	2.1	.15
Performance Management	32	41	26	1.5	1.9	1.9	.22*
Financial Transactions	30	53	18	—	1.6	1.9[1]	.08

Significance level: [t] $p \leq 0.10$ * $p \leq 0.05$ ** $p \leq 0.01$ *** $p \leq 0.001$

[1] Significant difference ($p \leq .05$) between 2001 and 2004.

Overall, it is clear that organizations are making greater use of self-service IT systems in the HR function, at least in the number of activities that are carried out on them. There will likely be continued growth both in the areas where individuals can service themselves via IT systems and in the number of companies that use such systems.

The relationship between the use of IT and HR's role in strategy is shown in Table 9.2. As a general rule, the relationships here are not strong, but some are statistically significant. Somewhat surprisingly, scheduling training, posting job openings, and changing addresses are all significantly related to HR's role in strategy. One explanation for this finding is that putting these operations on an IT self-service platform frees up HR to play an important role in strategy. It may also add credibility to HR, because HR has found a low-cost way to get some of this traditional work done.

It is surprising to find that some of the management tool items are not associated with HR playing a strategic role. Putting these types of tools in an IT system would, on the surface, appear to be a way to help HR play a bigger role in strategy because it makes human capital information much more accessible. It may be that the level of development in these areas is not high and, as a result, doing so would not enhance HR's role in strategy. It may also be that the level of sophistication required to be effective in these areas outstrips the capability of current IT systems and applications to deliver them effectively, so whether they are computerized has little relationship to HR's role in strategy.

Finally, it is interesting to note that the use of IT for performance management is significantly correlated with HR's role in strategy. This finding suggests that shifting more responsibility for performance management to managers and employees via IT tools is associated with HR's being more of a strategic partner. Not only may doing so enhance the general capability of employees and managers in this area, but it may provide a database of performance information that is helpful in strategy development and execution.

Strategic Focuses

Table 9.3 shows the relationship between the strategic focuses in an organization and the kinds of activities that are done on the computer. A number of significant relationships appear in this table. Not surprisingly, growth was found to be related to the use of IT for salary administration. Because one of the advantages of an IT-based salary administration system is scalability, it makes sense that such a system would be more likely to be used when growth is part of an organization's strategy. Scalability may also account for the correlation between growth and the ability to change personnel records by computer.

The core business strategic focus is found to be related to each of the IT system use items. One reason for this relationship may be that computerization is part of an effort by organizations to gain better control over their core businesses through simplifying and establishing standardized practices across the organization. Certainly computerization can drive standardization and scale-related cost-cutting, both of which are important in organizations that are focusing on core business.

Table 9.3. Relationship of Strategic Focuses to IT System Use

	Strategic Focuses					
Activities	Growth	Core Business	Quality and Speed	Information-Based Strategies	Knowledge-Based Strategies	Organizational Performance
Personal records	.24*	.25*	.04	.07	.22*	.14
Job information	.11	.24*	-.16	.05	.25*	.13
Employee training	.11	.32***	.03	.10	.30**	.36***
Management tools	.31**	.33***	.10	.20*	.36***	.41***
Salary administration	.34***	.23*	.18^t	.09	.27**	.24*
Performance management	.11	.19^t	.15	.15	.41***	.25*
Financial transactions	.11	.34***	-.16	.13	.13	.09

Significance level: ^{t} $p \le 0.10$ * $p \le 0.05$ ** $p \le 0.01$ *** $p \le 0.001$

Having knowledge-based strategies relates to almost all HR IT system uses. Organizations that are strongly focused on knowledge-based strategies need to do sophisticated human capital management, and having an IT system is one way to enable better management of human capital. Interestingly enough, the strongest correlation with knowledge-based strategy is in the area of performance management. This correlation may well reflect the new capabilities of some performance management systems to establish competency profiles for people throughout the organization; this capability is highly supportive of most knowledge-based business strategies.

Finally, the strategic focus of organizational performance is strongly related to four of the seven uses of IT systems. It is particularly interesting that the significant correlations were all in areas that move beyond personnel records, financial transactions, and job information. They include training, management tools, salary administration, and performance management, areas where there is potentially an impact not just on the efficiency of the HR organization, but also on the overall performance of the organization.

Conclusion

Overall, the relationships that we found between the strategic focuses of organizations and the use of IT systems highlight the fact that the non-transactional use of IT systems is related to business strategy. Knowledge and organizational performance strategies were particularly likely to be associated with the use of IT systems to support such critical human capital issues as performance management and training.

CHAPTER 10

Effectiveness of Information Systems

Our findings concerned with the effectiveness of HR IT systems are shown in Table 10.1. The table shows HR IT systems to be least effective when they provide management tools, and most effective when they involve personnel records and job information. Information technology-based systems have been used to carry out administrative activities for a longer time and, in most cases, these activities involve simple transactions. Thus it is not surprising that they are most effective at doing them.

Changes in Effectiveness

Comparing the effectiveness results of 1998 with those of 2004, we see four significant increases in effectiveness, and no significant decreases. The increases in the job information area are especially noteworthy. Apparently, IT job posting and job application processes have improved substantially. This improvement may be due to the emergence of service providers such as Monster.com and Brassring.com, which offer IT systems as part of their value proposition. For performance management and salary administration systems, there were small increases in effectiveness. Again, this result may reflect the fact that major vendors of HR systems such as SAP and Oracle as well as solution vendors have developed software in these areas.

In comparing the 2001 data with the 2004 data, we find that IT system effectiveness improved from 2001 to 2004; though none of the increases were large, there was an increase for nine of the activities. These results are generally encouraging, since they suggest that improvements occur as organizations become more experienced users of IT-based HR systems.

There were a few significant correlations between HR's role in strategy and the effectiveness of IT systems. Essentially, this finding was similar to our finding about the relationship between the utilization of information systems and HR's role in strategy. IT system effectiveness does not appear to have a major relationship to the role that HR plays in business strategy; exceptions to this are in the areas of job information provision and in managers' and employees' ability to obtain advice and information in handling personnel issues. It is interesting that providing information is more transactional, while obtaining advice is closer to strategic education on key practices. It may be that job information provision is an area that, when computerized, frees up HR to play a greater

Table 10.1. HR IT System Effectiveness

Activities	Percentages			Mean			
	Not Effective	Somewhat Effective	Very Effective	1998	2001	2004	Correlation with HR Role in Strategy
Personnel Records					2.6	2.7	.11
Change benefit coverage	2	34	64	2.5	2.6	2.6	.02
Change address and/or other personal information	0	28	72	2.4	2.5	2.7[1]	.13
Job Information					2.2	2.4	.33*
Apply for a job (external applicants)	2	55	43	2.1	2.4	2.4[1]	.13
Apply for a job (internal applicants)	2	53	45	1.8	2.4	2.4[1]	.15
Post job openings	5	49	46	2.3	2.5	2.4	.20[t]
Post personal resume/bio	19	55	26	—	1.8	2.1	.03
Employee Training					2.1	2.3	.18
New hire orientation	7	75	18	—	1.9	2.1	.07
Skills training	4	68	28	—	2.2	2.2	.12
Scheduling training	7	49	44	—	2.3	2.4	.12
Management Tools				—	—	2.1	-.01
Career development planning	21	67	12	1.7	1.8	1.9[1]	.26[t]
Obtain advice and information on handling personnel issues	9	89	2	1.8	1.9	1.9	.27*
Management development training	10	75	15	—	1.8	2.1	-.09
Search for employees with specified skills/competencies	25	60	15	—	1.7	1.9	.08
Assess skills/competencies/knowledge	25	66	9	—	—	1.8	.08
Access knowledge communities or experts	18	70	13	—	—	2.0	-.15
Access managers tool kit	5	73	22	—	—	2.2	.12
Salary Planning/Administration	4	59	37	2.2	2.4	2.3	.14
Performance Management	8	68	24	2.0	2.1	2.2	-.02
Financial Transactions	5	75	20	—	2.1	2.2	.06

Significance level: [t] $p \leq 0.10$ *$p \leq 0.05$ **$p \leq 0.01$ ***$p \leq 0.001$

[1] Significant difference ($p \leq .05$) between 1998 and 2004.

strategic role, whereas obtaining advice actually enhances the strategic capability of HR clients.

Table 10.2 relates the effectiveness of IT systems to a company's strategic focuses. We found relatively few significant results here, but there was one interesting result. Firms that pursue a strategy of quality and speed are more likely to have effective computer systems across a variety of dimensions, in particular for training. This correlation is understandable, given the focus on training that is present in most qual-

Table 10.2. Relationship of Strategic Focuses to IT System Effectiveness

IT SYSTEMS EFFECTIVENESS ON:	STRATEGIC FOCUSES					
	Growth	Core Business	Quality and Speed	Information-Based Strategies	Knowledge-Based Strategies	Organizational Performance
Personal records	-.06	.18	.08	-.00	-.02	.15
Job information	.38*	.18	.32*	.09	-.03	.17
Financial transactions	.10	.18	.12	.23^t	.20	.11
Employee training	.27^t	.21	.48***	.28^t	.19	.29^t
Management tools	.23^t	.24^t	.33*	.30*	.12	.36**
Salary administration	.17	.24*	.13	.07	.20^t	.12
Performance management	.13	.04	.28*	.16	.05	.19

Significance level: ^{t} $p \leq 0.10$ * $p \leq 0.05$ ** $p \leq 0.01$ *** $p \leq 0.001$

ity efforts and the ability of computer systems to deliver training and speed up processes.

IT System Effectiveness

Because of the relative newness of IT-based HR systems, there is relatively little information available about their overall effectiveness, or about their impact on the effectiveness of organizations and their HR systems. In order to measure effectiveness, beginning in 2001 we asked questions about both the effectiveness of IT-based HR systems in general and in specific areas. As can be seen in Table 10.3, a statistical factor analysis grouped the effectiveness questions into three clusters: employee satisfaction, efficiency, and business effectiveness.

The IT systems did not receive very high performance ratings on any of the outcomes. The highest ratings are in the areas of efficiency and employee satisfaction, but even there, the highest-rated item received a rating just barely above the middle of the rating scale. One positive note on the ratings of IT effectiveness, however, is that 45 percent of the respondents reported that the systems do not alienate their employees. Employee alienation is a concern of some HR professionals, apprehensive that the human touch may be replaced by impersonal computerized services.

It is hardly surprising that high ratings come in the efficiency area, since efficiency is an area where short-term payoffs should be achieved by an IT system. Nevertheless, it is significant that we now have data that con-

Table 10.3. Extent of HR IT System Effectiveness

Outcomes	Percentages					Mean		Correlation with HR Role in Strategy
	Little or No Extent	Some Extent	Moderate Extent	Great Extent	Very Great Extent	2001	2004	
Overall Effectiveness	6	27	40	25	1	**2.6**	**2.9**[1]	.18[t]
Employee Satisfaction						**3.0**	**3.0**	.16
Satisfy your employees	8	38	35	18	1	2.4	2.7	.17[t]
Build employee loyalty	36	31	25	6	1	2.0	2.0	.20*
Alienate employees [2]	45	41	11	2	1	1.4	1.7[1]	.05
Efficiency						**2.9**	**3.0**	.21*
Improve HR services	8	22	33	32	4	3.0	3.0	.17[t]
Reduce HR transaction costs	7	30	27	26	11	2.9	3.0	.17[t]
Speed up HR processes	5	21	28	39	7	3.1	3.2	.12
Reduce the number of employees in HR	24	24	27	20	5	2.4	2.6	.21*
Business Effectiveness						**2.2**	**2.3**	.19[t]
Provide new strategic information	34	27	20	19	0	2.1	2.3	.02
Support strategic change	32	24	22	20	2	2.3	2.4	.10
Integrate different HR processes (e.g., training, compensation)	28	24	32	14	2	2.4	2.4	.11
Enable the analysis of HR's impact on the business	37	26	27	9	1	2.1	2.1	.11
Produce a balanced scorecard of HR's effectiveness	39	28	19	11	3	1.9	2.1	.25*
Enable analysis of workforce characteristics	21	31	25	19	4	2.5	2.5	.23*
Provide a competitive advantage	32	33	22	9	3	2.2	2.2	.09

[1] Significant difference ($p \leq 05$) between 2001 and 2004.

[2] Scale is reversed for inclusion in the employee satisfaction scale.

Significance level: [t] $p \leq 0.10$ * $p \leq 0.05$ ** $p \leq 0.01$ *** $p \leq 0.001$

firm that the systems do, to some extent, improve HR services, reduce costs, and increase speed.

The lowest ratings come in business effectiveness, an area where there is reason to believe computer systems have the potential to affect the degree to which HR is a business partner. So far, however, HR executives do not see these systems strongly affecting organizational performance, strategic organizational change, or change management, perhaps in part due to the newness of the systems and the fact that organizations are just beginning to learn how to use IT systems as a strategic tool.

Only time will tell whether IT systems can make a positive contribution to organizational effectiveness. As Boudreau and Ramstad (2003) have noted, a decision science for HR remains elusive yet it is essential for guiding decision makers through the increasingly daunting amount of information available in HR IT systems. They note that having such a decision science is one reason that data systems in finance, marketing, supply-chain, and other areas have been so influential. As the HR profession develops a deeper and more precise decision science, IT systems may become more effective.

A comparison between the 2001 and 2004 data shows some positive movement in the ratings of IT-based HR systems. Overall effectiveness of the systems is rated significantly higher in 2004, and eight of the individual effectiveness items increased. Perhaps the best conclusion we can reach is that the performance of IT systems has improved from 2001 to 2004, but primarily in HR operations; we still await breakthroughs in driving business effectiveness.

The relationships between the effectiveness measures of HR IT systems and the role of HR in strategy are also shown in Table 10.3. They are consistently positive but in some cases are not statistically significant. It is interesting that greater efficiency does seem to be associated with a more important role in strategy. Perhaps more interesting is the significant relationship between two business effectiveness items, "produce a balanced scorecard of HR's effectiveness" and "enable analysis of workforce characteristics," and HR's role in strategy. These applications have received a good deal of attention in the management literature and are often strongly desired by line managers. This finding suggests that the HR system's ability to provide information that is desired by its managers may enable HR to play a more active role in strategy.

Strategic Focuses

As we see in Table 10.4, there are a number of significant relationships existing between IT effectiveness and the strategic focuses. All six of the

Table 10.4. Relationship of Strategic Focuses to HR IT Effectiveness

HR IT Outcomes	STRATEGIC FOCUS					
	Growth	Core Business	Quality and Speed	Information-Based Strategies	Knowledge-Based Strategies	Organizational Performance
Overall Effectiveness	.20*	.35***	.10	.10	.09	.23*
Employee Satisfaction	.30**	.22*	.18^t	.22*	.13	.36***
Efficiency	.29**	.33***	.21*	.04	.15	.28**
Business Effectiveness	.24*	.29**	.28**	.22*	.27**	.33***

Significance level: ^{t} $p \leq 0.10$ * $p \leq 0.05$ ** $p \leq 0.01$ *** $p \leq 0.001$

strategic focuses show some significant relationships, with three of them showing strong relationship for all the outcomes.

If an organization has a strategic focus on growth, core business, or organizational performance, HR executives are more likely to rate its computerized HR IT system positively than if it does not. Having a strong strategic focus, almost regardless of what that focus may be, appears to lead to greater satisfaction with the outcomes produced by the HR IT system. One possible explanation is that HR IT systems in organizations with clear strategic focuses are designed to support those focuses and, as a result, produce more satisfying results. This interpretation is supported by the fact that many of the strongest correlations in Table 10.4 are with business effectiveness. It is also supported by the argument that when an organization has a clear strategy, it can create an information system that actually produces better operating results.

Effectiveness and Use

Table 10.5 shows the relationship between the effectiveness of HR IT systems and the extent to which computer systems are used for a number of activities. As in 2001, in 2004 the relationships are consistently positive. Overall HR IT effectiveness is shown to be related to greater use of IT systems, for virtually all the activities studied. Efficiency is related to using systems for most activities, as is business effectiveness.

The relationships are particularly strong between business effectiveness and using IT systems for management tools and employee training. This is an interesting mix of transactional and competency-oriented applications. It is also notable that the use of IT systems for financial transactions is found to be largely unrelated to any of the effectiveness measures, suggesting that HR IT effectiveness may be driven by delivering

Table 10.5. Relationship of HR IT Effectiveness to HR IT System Use

HR IT Outcomes	Use HR IT Systems for:						
	Personal Records	Job Information	Financial Transactions	Employee Training	Management Tools	Salary / Planning Administration	Performance Management
Overall Effectiveness	.23*	.31**	.18^t	.47***	.56***	.26**	.23*
Employee Satisfaction	.20*	.23*	.19^t	.38***	.54***	.34***	.16
Efficiency	.39***	.37***	.16	.49***	.50***	.36***	.22*
Business Effectiveness	.19^t	.27**	.16	.42***	.60***	.28**	.33***

Significance level:　　^{t} $p \leq 0.10$　　* $p \leq 0.05$　　** $p \leq 0.01$　　*** $p \leq 0.001$

more than just efficient transaction processing. Generally, the results suggest that the more HR IT systems are seen as effective, the more use they receive.

Table 10.6 shows the relationship of HR IT system effectiveness to the degree of information technology use. There clearly is a strong relationship here in 2004, as there was in 2001. Completely integrated human resource information systems are rated much higher on overall IT effectiveness, efficiency, and business effectiveness. Less strongly related is employee satisfaction.

The strong relationships to effectiveness undoubtedly reflect the power that integrated systems have. They offer the opportunity to do many more things with the HR IT system—in particular, to do analyses related to business effectiveness and business strategy. For example, it is possible to assess the practicality of a business strategy by determining whether the organization has the capability to execute it. It is also possible to determine the impacts of HR programs and to more effectively develop and reward employees.

Conclusion

Our findings bear out that HR IT systems are most effective at providing transaction tools for HR administrations. When combined with the data on usage we reported in Chapter 9, we can see that HR IT systems are most frequently used to do the things that they do best.

Overall, HR IT systems are rated as not much more effective in 2004 than they were in 2001, and they are not rated as very effective in an absolute sense. There are many possible reasons for this result, including the fact that they are relatively new and that companies are just beginning to learn how to utilize them effectively. The technology is

Table 10.6. Relationship of HR IT Effectiveness to State of HR IT

HR IT Outcomes	HR IT[1]
Overall Effectiveness	.43***
Employee Satisfaction	.27**
Efficiency	.38***
Business Effectiveness	.38***

Significance level: [t] $p \le 0.10$ * $p \le 0.05$ ** $p \le 0.01$ *** $p \le 0.001$

[1]Response scale: 5 = Completely integrated HR information technology system;
4 = Most processes are information technology–based but not fully integrated;
3 = Some HR processes are information technology–based;
2 = Little information technology present in the HR function;
1 = No information technology present

advancing rapidly, and many companies may be experiencing difficulties dealing with a technology that is not well developed.

The evidence is quite clear that HR IT systems are most effective when they fit the strategy of an organization. Perhaps the most consistent finding is that the more things the HR IT system can do and the more services it offers, the more effective it is perceived to be. Finally, systems are rated highest on effectiveness when they do HR transactions and provide management tools and training.

CHAPTER 11

HR Analytics and Metrics

Organizations can collect and make use of three major HR measurement types: measures of efficiency, effectiveness, and impact. All can be useful. Each calls for somewhat different metrics and analytics. They compliment each other, when they are used together.

Efficiency measures are most common. They are basic to the HR function, and they connect readily to the existing accounting system. There will likely be growing attention given to measuring effectiveness, by focusing on such things as turnover, attitudes, and bench strength. Rarely do organizations consider impact (for example, the relative effect of improving the quality of different talent pools on organizational effectiveness). More important, rarely is HR measurement specifically directed to vital talent "segments," where decisions are most important. As we noted in Chapter 5, the development of a logical decision science for human capital, talent, and organization effectiveness is very likely a requirement for progress to occur in such areas as strategic partnership, HR IT systems, and measurement and analytics.

Use and Relationship to HR Role in Business Strategy

Table 11.1 shows HR's use of metrics and analytics. The results suggest that measurement and analytics, though no longer in their infancy, remain relatively rare HR practices. No measurement elements are used by more than 50 percent of responding organizations. The areas of HR measurement that are used most (over 40 percent of organizations reporting "yes, have now") relate to measuring the efficiency of HR operations, creating traditional HR data benchmarks, and measuring the cost of HR services. Though these measurement areas are important, they primarily reflect "efficiency." They also reflect a traditional "service delivery" perspective, rather than the decision science perspective.

Beyond efficiency measures, use of metrics and analytics is rarer, with less than 40 percent of organizations reporting that they use the effectiveness and impact measures. This finding is similar to those of Lawler, Levenson, and Boudreau (2004) and Gates (2004).

In the middle range of use are metrics and analytics to track the effectiveness of outsourced HR activities, and dashboards or scorecards to evaluate HR's performance

The least-utilized areas of HR measurement and analytics are conducting cost-benefit analysis of HR programs, and measuring the effect of

Table 11.1. HR Metrics and Analytics Use

Practices	Percentages					
	Not Currently Being Considered	Planning For	Being Built	Yes, Have Now	MEAN	Correlation with HR Role in Strategy
Impact						
Collect metrics that measure the business impact of HR programs and processes?	17	27	25	30	2.7	.20*
Effectiveness						
Use dashboards or scorecards to evaluate HR's performance?	14	23	23	39	2.9	.31**
Use measures and analytics to evaluate and track the performance of outsourced HR activities?	23	24	14	38	2.7	.30**
Have metrics and analytics that reflect the effects of HR programs on the workforce (such as, competence, motivation, attitudes, behaviors, etc.)?	18	27	25	29	2.7	.29**
Have the capability to conduct cost-benefit analyses (also called utility analyses) of HR programs?	24	30	17	28	2.5	.19^t
Efficiency						
Measure the financial efficiency of HR operations (e.g., cost-per-hire, time-to-fill, training costs)?	9	19	24	47	3.1	.29**
Collect metrics that measure the cost of providing HR services?	12	21	25	41	3.0	.24*
Benchmark analytics and measures against data from outside organizations (e.g., Saratoga, Mercer, Hewitt, etc.)?	11	25	15	48	3.0	.11

Response scale reversed from survey order: 1 = not currently being considered, 2 = planning for, 3 = being built, 4 = yes, have now

Significance level: ^{t} $p \leq 0.10$ * $p \leq 0.05$ ** $p \leq 0.01$ *** $p \leq 0.001$

HR programs on employees. Cost-benefit analysis has often been referred to as the "holy grail" of HR measurement, and it certainly has drawn the attention of many HR leaders and consultants. Understanding the ROI of HR programs is useful, but doing so may tell little about the synergies among HR programs and the overall value of measures in enhancing decisions about human capital. A combination of efficiency, effectiveness, and impact measures is likely to emerge as the most effective approach, but this combination clearly has not yet developed in most organizations.

The question about measuring "the business impact of HR programs and processes" shows a low adoption rate. This situation may not change soon. Our experience suggests that when HR leaders are asked about measuring "business impact," they often interpret it to mean the effects of specific programs on workforce changes such as skills, competencies, and attitudes, rather than the effects of such programs on business outcomes such as financial targets and competitive sustainability.

The relationship of the use of HR metrics to HR's role in strategy is shown in the right-hand column of Table 11.1. Almost all of the measurement items are significantly positively correlated with greater HR involvement in strategy. The one exception is the use of benchmarks, which shows no significant relationship to HR strategy involvement. That weak relationship may reflect the fact that benchmarks have become so ubiquitous that they no longer lead to strategic involvement for HR.

However, some measurement elements, particularly dashboards and financial efficiency, are both relatively common and have strong correlations with HR involvement in strategy. Thus, for benchmarks it appears that the lack of relationship is not necessarily due to their commonness. Rather, it may be that benchmarks simply do not provide a significant platform for strategic involvement. Benchmarking can be useful for helping HR to understand where HR activities are so inefficient as to be clearly non-competitive. However, strategic success often depends on unique, protectable, and sustainable advantages, something that cannot be determined by benchmarking.

As for the other measurement elements, the fact that their existence and use is uniformly related to HR's strategic involvement, and that many of them remain relatively rare, suggests there is great potential to use HR measures to enhance strategic human capital decisions. Although it is not possible to determine causality, our belief is that these findings reflect a combination, with metrics being both a precursor and a result of HR strategic involvement.

That virtually all of the measurement items have similar and statistically significant relationships with HR's involvement in business strategy supports Boudreau and Ramstad's proposition (1997, 2003, 2005a, 2006) that the most effective measurement systems combine impact, effectiveness, and efficiency. The fact that some of the more common measurement elements (scorecards and efficiency measures) have somewhat higher correlations suggests that their commonality also carries some credibility with business leaders. If this is the case, then there may be a potential for HR leaders to become more effective by using and communicating the value of the less-common HR measures (such as measures of the impact of HR programs on business success or cost-benefit analysis of HR programs), which are also related to strategic involvement.

Table 11.2. HR Metrics and Analytics Use and Strategic Focuses

Practices	Strategic Focuses					
	Growth	Core Business	Quality and Speed	Information-Based Strategies	Knowledge-Based Strategies	Organizational Performance
Impact						
Collect metrics that measure the business impact of HR programs and processes?	.20^t	.12	.29**	.36***	.30**	.30**
Effectiveness						
Use dashboards or scorecards to evaluate HR's performance?	.20^t	.20*	.15	.23*	.27**	.21*
Use measures and analytics to evaluate and track the performance of outsourced HR activities?	.11	.29**	.04	.10	.12	.16
Have metrics and analytics that reflect the effects of HR programs on the workforce (such as, competence, motivation, attitudes, behaviors, etc.)?	.05	.16	.15	.15	.07	.21*
Have the capability to conduct cost-benefit analyses (also called utility analyses) of HR programs?	.15	.22*	.27**	.16	.30**	.25*
Efficiency						
Measure the financial efficiency of HR operations (e.g. cost-per-hire, time-to-fill, training costs)?	.04	.15	.12	.09	.15	.23*
Collect metrics that measure the cost of providing HR services?	.26**	.20^t	.18^t	.20*	.25*	.28**
Benchmark analytics and measures against data from outside organizations (e.g., Saratoga, Mercer, Hewitt, etc.)?	-.03	.12	-.04	.05	-.01	.11

Significance level: ^{t} $p \leq 0.10$ * $p \leq 0.05$ ** $p \leq 0.01$ *** $p \leq 0.001$

Use of Metrics and Analytics Related to Strategic Focus

Table 11.2 shows the relationship between the use of HR measurement systems and the strategic focuses of the organization. The patterns suggest that growth and organization performance strategies are associated with very different HR measurement uses. They also provide some insights about the importance of impact, effectiveness, and efficiency.

The extent to which an organization pursues a growth strategy has no relationship to any of the measurement uses except the cost of providing HR services. In contrast, all of the measurement uses except benchmarking and tracking the performance of outsourced activities correlate significantly with the extent to which organizations pursued an organizational performance strategy.

The difference in the relationships between the pursuit of growth and organizational performance strategies may reflect that growth strategies drive a focus on a few business outcomes, making it possible to manage HR decisions adequately simply by tracking HR costs. In contrast, organizational performance strategies may reflect an attempt to find unique and unaddressed ways to enhance the effectiveness of mature businesses, and thus may require integrating many complex business elements and giving attention to finding overlooked opportunities. It is also possible that organizations that pursue organizational performance are more mature and have better-developed measurement systems.

The results for "quality/speed" are interesting, because it is the one strategy in which items reflecting a concern with the combination of cost and impact measurement are significant but items measuring efficiency and effectiveness are not. This outcome may reflect the possibility that a quality/speed focus often occurs within highly focused management frameworks such as total quality, that provide a logic for examining the correspondence between HR costs and benefits, and available accepted measures of business outcomes to relate to HR cost measures.

Some of the individual items reveal interesting patterns. Measuring the business impact of HR programs shows no relationship with pursuing growth and core business strategies, but strong and significant relationships with the other strategies. Perhaps growth and core business strategies present simpler strategic environments, and thus less demand for or payoff from measures that connect human capital practices to organizational performance.

Measuring the cost of HR services is significantly or marginally related to all strategic focuses. It appears that an increased attention to measuring HR costs is a common result of or precursor to a wide range of strategies.

HR Metrics and Analytics Effectiveness

Table 11.3 shows the results regarding the effectiveness of HR measurement systems in contributing to various aspects of functional and strategic success. The overall pattern is striking: for all but two of the outcomes, HR measurements are rated as effective or very effective by 30 percent or less of the respondents. The two exceptions are "assessing and improving HR department operations" and "supporting organiza-

Table 11.3. HR Metrics and Analytics Effectiveness

Outcomes	Percentages					Mean	Correlation with HR Role in Strategy
	Very Ineffective	Ineffective	Somewhat Effective	Effective	Very Effective		
Assessing HR programs before they are implemented — not just after they are operational	10	28	40	20	1	2.7	.18[t]
Pinpointing HR programs that should be discontinued	6	30	46	14	3	2.8	.14
Evaluating the effectiveness of most HR programs and practices	3	20	52	23	1	3.0	.34***
Assessing and improving the HR department operations	0	10	41	45	4	3.4	.16
Connecting human capital practices to organizational performance	10	30	51	8	1	2.6	.36***
Assessing and improving the human capital strategy of the company	2	27	44	23	4	3.0	.30**
Identifying where talent has the greatest potential for strategic impact	4	22	49	21	3	3.0	.37***
Contributing to decisions about business strategy and human capital management	2	33	37	23	4	2.9	.42***
Supporting organizational change efforts	3	11	45	35	5	3.3	.37***
Making decisions and recommendations that reflect your company's competitive situation	5	20	44	28	2	3.0	.43***
Assessing the feasibility of new business strategies	13	31	35	18	2	2.7	.43***

Significance level: [t] $p \leq 0.10$ * $p \leq 0.05$ ** $p \leq 0.01$ *** $p \leq 0.001$

tional change efforts." Only about 50 percent rate measures as effective or very effective for assessing and improving HR operations, and the positive rating is only 40 percent for supporting organizational change efforts.

Evaluating HR department operations is perhaps the most functionally focused and operationally specific effect on the list, whereas organization change is arguably focused on much broader outcomes involving constituents and considerations well beyond the HR function. Although "assessing and improving HR operations" is rated relatively highly for its effectiveness, the correlation between the effectiveness rating and HR's strategic involvement is not significant, suggesting that the value of such measures is related to areas other than strategic involvement. In contrast, "supporting organization change efforts" has a large and statistically significant association with HR's strategic involvement.

It may be that in many organizations, there is a well-developed organizational change group that is separate from and independent of the rest of HR, and has developed measurements specifically designed for its activities. It may also be that organization change efforts occur in the context of total quality or other frameworks that have existing strong measurement frameworks and tap into more strategically relevant business and financial measurement systems. If they do, there may be significant potential strategic value for HR leaders to tap into these measurement systems for other purposes besides organization change.

Most of the remaining items are rated as effective or very effective by from 20 percent to 30 percent of companies. The lowest-rated items are "connecting human capital practices to organizational performance" and "pinpointing HR programs that should be discontinued." Both of these reflect a common theme—the ability to clearly measure HR's impact and act on that information proactively.

The vast majority of items show a strong and significant correlation between rated effectiveness and HR's involvement in strategy. High correlations are found for "making decisions and recommendations that reflect your company's competitive situation," "assessing the feasibility of new business strategies" and "contributing to decisions about business strategy and human capital management." Notably non- or marginally significant are "assessing HR programs before they are implemented—not just after they are operational," "pinpointing HR programs that should be discontinued," and "assessing and improving the HR department operations."

The items with the three most highly significant correlations reflect decidedly business and competitive strategy purposes, whereas those with the three least significant correlations reflect internal HR functional purposes. This suggests that although improving the effectiveness of measures that focus within the HR function may be valuable, it may not lead to greater strategic involvement.

We often encounter HR and business leaders who believe that the HR profession must first "get its own house in order," by improving measurement of, and achieving, its own functional effectiveness, and that only after doing so should it focus on strategic effectiveness. The results reported here suggest that the two types of measurement effectiveness operate independently. This supports the idea of developing HR measurement systems that are strategically relevant, even before perfecting measurement systems that assess the HR function.

Conclusion

Overall, the results suggest that HR measurement and analytics are underdeveloped and are significantly related to HR's role in strategy. The growing attention to HR metrics and analytics seems well placed, considering the potential for improvement and value. It is also important to note that all measurement elements are not equally valuable. It appears that measures that are often thought to be related to HR effectiveness and strategic influence (such as benchmarking) are actually not related to it. On the other hand, an "intermediate" set of measures (such as scorecards and HR program effects) appears to offer opportunities to enhance HR strategic influence. There also appears to be an emerging measurement emphasis on impact, which is not yet well understood. It has a weaker but still significant relationship with HR's strategic involvement. HR and business leaders are likely to find that the most effective measurement systems combine efficiency, effectiveness, and impact—a pattern that appears to be emerging generally, and is particularly evident in organizations with a strategic focus on organizational performance.

CHAPTER 12

Human Resource Skills

In a knowledge economy, the knowledge and skill requirements for the members of an organization's staff functions continually evolve, just as they do for the firm's core business and technical units. A company's business model changes in order to increase the value the company delivers to its customers. The business model of the human resource function, too, must change in order for it to continue to support corporate performance. Doing so requires HR to develop new capabilities as a function and HR professionals with new knowledge and skills.

Skill Satisfaction

Table 12.1 shows the level of satisfaction with the skills that often are required in today's human resource function. Satisfaction with skills factored into five areas: (1) HR technical skills (new in 2004); (2) organizational dynamics; (3) business partner; (4) administrative; and (5) metrics (new in 2004).

Not surprisingly, the highest level of satisfaction is with HR technical skills. The next highest levels of satisfaction are with skills that pertain to organizational dynamics, including interpersonal skills, team skills, consulting, coaching, and leadership/management skills. Satisfaction with administrative skills is mixed. Record-keeping skills are seen positively. However, respondents are neutral about skills in managing contractors and vendors. This is a skill that has increased in importance in today's world, where outsourcing is central to being able to carry out the HR role.

A low level of satisfaction exists with business partner skills. There has been a significant increase in business understanding since 1998. However, deficits are still perceived in the substantive business support areas of strategic planning and organization design, and in cross-functional and global understanding. Satisfaction with change management skills remains in the neutral range.

Although HR professionals may increasingly understand the business, they still do not appear to bring substantive business expertise to the table. This deficit clearly has to change if HR is to influence strategic and organizational direction. It is a critical weakness with respect to HR's performing as an effective business partner. Evidence from our results on metrics and the HR decision science suggests that fixing this deficit may require going well beyond simple business acumen or finance and marketing classes; a truly unique perspective must be created that sees strategy through the lens of HR and human capital.

Table 12.1. Satisfaction with Current Skills of the HR Staff

Skills	Percentages					Mean			
	Very Dissatisfied	Dissatisfied	Neutral	Satisfied	Very Satisfied	1995	1998	2001	2004
HR Technical Skills									**3.8**
HR technical skills	0	5	17	48	30	—	—	—	4.0
Process execution and analysis	1	12	36	38	12	—	—	—	3.5
Organizational Dynamics						**3.2**	**3.1**	**3.6**	**3.7**[1]
Team skills	1	4	27	56	12	3.3	3.2	3.7	3.7[1]
Consultation skills	1	12	37	41	9	3.0	2.9	3.4	3.4[1]
Coaching and facilitation	3	8	36	40	13	3.2	3.1	3.4	3.5[1]
Leadership/management skills	1	8	40	41	10	3.1	2.9	3.3	3.5[1]
Interpersonal skills	0	2	13	59	26	3.7	3.5	4.0	4.1[1]
Business Partner Skills						—	—	—	**3.2**
Business understanding	1	13	42	38	6	3.0	2.9	3.3	3.3[1]
Strategic planning	5	29	36	26	5	—	2.8	2.9	3.0
Organizational design	5	20	41	31	3	—	2.7	2.9	3.1
Change management	1	21	35	37	6	—	—	3.2	3.3
Cross-functional experience	5	26	43	22	4	2.9	2.8	2.9	2.9
Global understanding	7	32	41	17	3	—	2.6	2.7	2.8
Communications	1	2	33	48	16	—	—	—	3.8
Administrative Skills						—	—	**3.4**	**3.5**
Record keeping	1	4	34	48	13	3.6	3.6	3.7	3.7
Managing contractors / vendors	4	11	42	38	5	—	3.2	3.3	3.3
Metrics Skills						—	—	—	**2.8**
Information technology	3	22	47	24	4	—	—	3.1	3.0
Metrics development	7	43	31	15	4	—	—	—	2.7
Data analysis and mining	8	38	27	24	4	—	—	—	2.8

Note: Items with means indicated by (—) were not asked

[1] Significant difference ($p \le .05$) between 1995 and 2004.

As in 2001, there is relatively low satisfaction with information technology skills. Apparently, HR managers still need to improve in this area. The area of greatest dissatisfaction concerns metrics development, and data analysis and mining. This area is particularly critical in terms of the ability of the HR function to play a major business strategic role.

Table 12.2. HR Professionals with Necessary Skill Set

Have Skills	Percentages				
	1995	1998	2001	2004	
				HR Executives	Managers
None	0	0	0	0	0
1 – 20%	0	2	5	2	5
21 – 40%	19	15	19	12	17
41 – 60%	35	39	33	37	28
61 – 80%	37	40	33	34	37
81 – 99%	9	4	10	11	13
100%	1	0	0	3	0
Mean	**4.4**	**4.3**	**4.3**	**4.5**	**4.3**

Mean; scale response: 1 = none; 2 = 1–20%; 3 = 21–40%; 4 = 41–60%; 5 = 61–80%; 6 = 81–99%; 7 = 100%

Bringing in data and doing data analysis are critical in many business decisions; thus, it is particularly important that HR executives develop good skill sets in these areas.

The level of satisfaction remained relatively constant from 1995 to 1998, but there was a significant improvement in satisfaction with several skill areas from 1998 to 2004. This increase in satisfaction is most evident with respect to organizational dynamics skills. Also significantly improving was business understanding, a key skill with respect to HR being a strategic partner.

Despite the improvement in satisfaction with skills in some areas, as we see in Table 12.2, the percentage of HR professionals and managers with the necessary overall skills did not change significantly from 1995 to 2004. Very few HR executives report that over 80 percent of their staff have the necessary skills. The same conclusion is reached by the line managers, who give a slightly lower appraisal of the skills of HR professionals.

Apparently the areas of low skill satisfaction (Table 12.1) are viewed as important in the overall skill portfolio of the HR function. Thus, although skill development progress was made in the more traditional areas of HR expertise and in organizational dynamics, many HR professionals have not yet developed satisfactory skills.

Table 12.3 presents data about skill satisfaction, comparing the responses of HR executives with those of other managers. It yields a rather surpris-

Table 12.3. Satisfaction with Skills and Knowledge of HR Professional

Skills	HR Executives		Managers		Satisfaction Correlation of HR Executives with Managers
	Mean	Correlation with HR Role in Strategy	Mean	Correlation with HR Role in Strategy	
HR Technical Skills	**3.8**	**.47*****	**3.9[1]**	**.18**	**.48*****
HR technical skills	4.0	.44***	4.1	.13	.39**
Process execution and analysis	3.5	.33***	3.6	.18	.30*
Organizational Dynamics	**3.7**	**.39*****	**3.8**	**.36****	**.47*****
Team skills	3.7	.50***	3.9	.26*	.41***
Consultation skills	3.4	.20[t]	3.7[1]	.19[t]	.29*
Coaching and facilitation	3.5	.30**	3.6	.39***	.34**
Leadership/management skills	3.5	.29**	3.6	.40***	.34**
Interpersonal skills	4.1	.28**	4.0	.26*	.35**
Business Partner Skills	**3.2**	**.31****	**3.5[1]**	**.37****	**.43*****
Business understanding	3.3	.10	3.5	.31**	.14
Strategic planning	3.0	.31**	3.2	.46***	.36**
Organizational design	3.1	.27**	3.6[1]	.24*	.29*
Change management	3.3	.33***	3.6[1]	.23*	.49***
Cross-functional experience	2.9	.08	3.2	.15	.33**
Global understanding	2.8	.25*	3.3[1]	.18	.40**
Communications	3.8	.28**	3.8	.31**	.32**
Administrative Skills	**3.5**	**.17[t]**	**3.5**	**.19**	**.34****
Record keeping	3.7	.18[t]	3.7	.23*	.29*
Managing contractors / vendors	3.3	.10	3.4	.06	.19
Metrics Skills	**2.8**	**.21***	**3.1[1]**	**.17**	**.60*****
Information technology	3.0	.07	3.1	.09	.39**
Metrics development	2.7	.23*	3.2[1]	.31**	.40***
Data analysis and mining	2.8	.23*	3.0[1]	-.01	.42***

Scale response: 1 = very dissatisfied; 2 = dissatisfied; 3 = neither; 4 = satisfied; 5 = very satisfied

[1] Significant difference ($p \leq .05$) between HR executives and managers.

Significance level: [t] $p \leq 0.10$ * $p \leq 0.05$ ** $p \leq 0.01$ *** $p \leq 0.001$

ing result: overall, HR executives are actually more dissatisfied with the skills of the HR staff than are other managers. Apparently, HR is harder on itself than others are. We have no evidence about the cause of this pattern, but it may be that HR suffers from a bit of an inferiority complex, because it is often on the defensive and criticized by others in the organization.

The differences between the views of HR managers and the other managers is particularly striking in the area of metrics. Managers rate HR as significantly more skillful vis-à-vis metrics development and data analysis mining than do HR executives. We suspect that this result may arise in part because managers have low expectations and may be impressed with the mere existence of measures, data, and scorecards. HR executives, in contrast, may be better able to see the untapped potential in such systems. Other areas where there are major gaps include organizational design, change management, and global understanding.

In general, business partner skill areas are rated lower by HR executives than they are by managers. This may be one area where HR underestimates its skills, and it may help explain why HR often is not a business partner. What may be needed to develop HR further as a business partner is for it to realize that it often has something to contribute in this area and that others see it as capable of adding value. Perhaps it needs to knock on the business partner door more often. Our data suggest that if it does so, HR is likely to find a more favorable reception than it expects.

Role in Strategy

The relationship between HR skill satisfaction and HR's role in strategy is shown in Table 12.3. Let's look first at the correlations for the HR executives' data. The correlations for HR technical skills, organizational dynamics, business partner skills, and metrics skills are all significant. Administrative skills and the item referring to information technology are less strongly related to HR's role in strategy.

The very high correlations between technical skills and HR's role in strategy support the view that HR technical skills are required in order to get involved in business strategy. The correlations between organizational dynamics and business partner skills were expected to be high, given that they are truly the foundation for contributing to business strategy, both for implementation and development. Perhaps the most surprising correlation is for the business understanding item; it shows no correlation with HR's role in strategy.

A somewhat different picture of the relationship of HR skills and HR's role in strategy exists in the data from managers. Perhaps not surprisingly, HR technical skills are not significantly related to managers' perceptions of HR strategy involvement. This is one piece of evidence that suggests HR technical mastery is not that important to being involved with strategy. Not surprisingly, the organizational design skills and business partner skills are significantly related to managers' perceptions of HR being involved with strategy. Unlike the finding for HR managers, business understanding is highly related to being a strategic partner. This result is more easily explainable than the result for HR managers. It is hard to imagine business managers wanting an HR executive to be involved without a good understanding of the business.

Overall, our findings about the relationship of skill satisfaction and strategic role strongly suggest that organizational dynamic skills and business partner skills are critical to HR being a business partner. Less important—at least in the findings for HR executives—but still relevant, are administrative skills.

The last column in Table 12.3 shows the correlation between HR skill satisfaction as expressed by managers and as expressed by HR executives. As we would expect, most of the correlations are statistically significant.

One low correlation is for managing contractors and vendors, an area that is not easily observable by managers not in HR. The lowest correlation concerns the level of business understanding of the HR professional community. This low correlation may very well explain why there is a relatively low correlation between business understanding satisfaction on the part of the HR executives and the degree to which HR is involved in business strategy. HR executives and managers may simply have different ideas of what business skills are needed. The result is that HR is not participating as much as it feels it should in the business strategy process. One implication of this is that HR needs to have a better understanding of what the rest of the organization focuses on in judging how knowledgeable the HR function is about business issues. HR then needs to be sure it has the appropriate knowledge and that the rest of the organization is aware of it.

Strategic Focuses

The relationship between strategic focuses and HR skill satisfaction is shown in Table 12.4. There are a number of positive correlations, particularly with respect to business partner skills, HR technical skills, and organizational dynamic skills. They are all associated with three or more of the strategic focuses. Administrative skill satisfaction relates only to information-based strategies. This correlation may be due to the need to reliably administer HR data in such organizations. Interestingly, HR

Table 12.4. Relationship of Strategic Focuses to HR Skills Satisfaction

Skills	Strategic Focuses					
	Growth	Core Business	Quality and Speed	Information-Based Strategies	Knowledge-Based Strategies	Organizational Performance
HR Technical Skills	.21*	.20*	.23*	.15	.29**	.28**
Organizational Dynamics	.23*	.07	.35***	.23*	.25*	.24*
Business Partner Skills	.14	.06	.38***	.23*	.26**	.18^t
Administrative Skills	-.01	.09	.10	.23*	.09	-.01
Metrics Skills	.05	.15	.14	.19^t	.13	.20*

Significance level: ^{t} $p \leq 0.10$ * $p \leq 0.05$ ** $p \leq 0.01$ *** $p \leq 0.001$

technical skill satisfaction is significant for all focuses *except* information-based.

Overall, organizations with stronger strategic focuses tend to have HR functions with better skill sets. This situation seems to be particularly true for organizations with organizational performance, knowledge-based, quality and speed, and information-based strategic focuses. It is easy to see why knowledge-based or organizational-performance focuses would lead to better skills in the HR area. They often require HR functions that are not only able to execute their technical skills but also to design systems that support organizational performance and knowledge development and utilization. The same is often true of quality and speed as a strategic focus. It takes a particular type of HR system to support this strategic initiative. Having a strategic focus also may make it easier for the HR function to develop the right skills and focus.

Conclusion

The results suggest that HR suffers from a skills deficit. It is notable that there is only a moderate level of satisfaction with all HR skills (no rating was higher than 4.1 on a 5-point scale), and that most ratings fall into the neutral category. Of particular concern are the relatively low ratings given to business partner skills, since they are related to HR's playing a significant role in strategy. On the encouraging side there has been an improvement in organizational dynamics skills. Still, there is much work to be done to enhance HR skills as well as develop a common understanding about the nature and level of those skills.

CHAPTER 13

Effectiveness of the HR Organization

The overall effectiveness of an HR organization must be based upon its performance in a number of areas. The most obvious area is service delivery. To be an effective business partner, HR also has to support current business performance. Finally, to operate effectively as a strategic partner, it needs to deliver value with respect to business strategy, organizational change, and human capital decision making.

Effectiveness Trends

Our respondents were asked to judge the overall effectiveness of their HR organizations and to judge their effectiveness in fourteen areas. As shown in Table 13.1, our statistical factor analysis produced three groups of effectiveness items: corporate roles, services, and business strategy and change.

The results for HR executives showed higher ratings for 2004 than in 1995, 1998, and 2001. Apparently, HR feels it is doing a better job than it has in the past. In all four time periods, the effectiveness ratings by HR executives are highest for the provision of HR services. This is also true of the 2004 ratings from managers. This finding is consistent with other studies, which have found that HR tends to be rated particularly highly when it comes to the delivery of basic HR services (Csoka and Hackett, 1998).

HR receives a particularly low rating for analytics. This low rating probably reflects the newness of this activity, as well as its complexity. Another low-rated activity is helping to develop business strategies. Managers rated this the lowest, and it must change if HR is to become a strategic partner.

In two HR service activities—providing HR services and tailoring practices to fit business needs—managers give HR performance a significantly lower rating than HR executives did. This finding suggests that HR may be overestimating how effective it is as a provider of HR services.

Both HR executives and other managers rate performance of corporate roles highly as a performance area for the HR function. Most highly rated is outsourcing and working with the corporate board. HR executives and managers are similar in how they perceive HR effectiveness in performing its corporate roles. Only one item, operating centers of excellence, shows a statistically significant difference, with HR executives rating their performance more highly.

Table 13.1. Effectiveness of HR Organization

Activities	1995	1998	2001	HR Executives 2004	Correlation with HR Role in Strategy	Managers 2004	Correlation with HR Role in Strategy	Effectiveness Correlations of HR Executives with Managers
Overall Effectiveness				6.9	.38**	6.7	.17	.60***
HR Services				7.0	.39***	6.8	.31**	.56***
Providing HR services	7.2	7.0	7.3	7.8	.18^t	7.2^1	.22^t	.39**
Tailoring human resource practices to fit business needs	6.9	6.9	6.7	7.1	.22*	6.4^1	.35**	.27*
Helping shape a viable employment relationship for the future	—	5.8	6.4	6.9	.34***	6.5	.38***	.42***
Being an employee advocate	—	6.8	7.2	7.4	.39***	7.3	.24*	.34**
Analyzing HR and business metrics	—	—	—	5.9	.32**	6.4	.10	.64***
Corporate Roles				6.9	.33**	6.8	-.05	.41*
Managing outsourcing of transactional services (e.g., benefits)	—	6.5	6.4	7.4^2	.13	6.9	-.05	.45***
Managing outsourcing of HR expertise (e.g., compensation design)	—	6.2	6.0	7.1^2	.20^t	6.7	-.18	.32*
Operating HR centers of excellence	—	5.5	5.6	6.8^2	.25*	6.0^1	.07	.43***
Operating HR shared service units	—	5.7	6.0	6.9^2	.35***	6.5	.05	.37**
Working with the corporate board	—	—	—	7.1	.50***	7.1	.35**	.35*
Business and Strategy				6.5	.51***	6.3	.40***	.51***
Providing change consulting services	5.8	5.5	5.7	6.5^2	.37***	6.1	.31**	.41***
Being a business partner	6.3	6.5	6.4	7.1^2	.46***	6.8	.42***	.43***
Helping to develop business strategies	—	6.2	5.8	6.0	.56***	5.7	.42***	.51***
Improving decisions about human capital	—	—	—	6.7	.24*	6.7	.39***	.29*

Scale response: 1 = not meeting needs, 10 = all needs met.

Note: Items with means indicated by (—) were not asked.

[1] Significant difference ($p \leq .05$) between HR executives and managers.

[2] Significant difference ($p \leq .05$) between 2001 and 2004

Significance level: ^{t} $p \leq 0.10$ * $p \leq 0.05$ ** $p \leq 0.01$ *** $p \leq 0.001$

The ratings by both HR executives and managers are lowest in regard to developing business strategy. However, being a business partner is rated relatively highly. This finding supports the point made in Chapter 1, that there is a difference between being a business partner and having an active role in strategy development. When managers consider successful business partnerships, they do not seem to see it as synonymous with an active role in developing business strategies. One final way to look at the scores on effectiveness concerns their absolute level. The ratings are on a ten-point scale; thus, even the highest ratings, 7.8 for HR executives and 7.3 for managers, fall significantly short of the top of the scale. Clearly, there is still plenty of room for HR to improve its effectiveness.

The final column of Table 13.1 shows the correlation between effectiveness ratings by HR executives and those by managers. They are all statistically significant, and many of them are quite high (above .50). It appears that HR executives and others in the organization are generally in agreement about how effectively the HR organization performs. In some respects, this is an encouraging note for the HR function. It indicates that in an important area the HR function is in touch with how its clients see its performance. This offers a good basis for a dialogue about what improvements the function can make in its performance. Nonetheless, the majority of the correlations are below .50, suggesting areas where there could be greater clarity about the meaning and level of effectiveness.

Role in Strategy

Table 13.1 also shows the correlations between the role that HR plays in strategy and its effectiveness. There are a number of relatively large correlations here, with respect to the data from both the HR executives and the managers. Not surprisingly, the strongest pattern of relationships has to do with the effectiveness of HR performance in the business strategy area. The more effective HR is in this area, the more it is seen as a business strategy partner.

In the data from both HR executives and managers, effectiveness in providing HR services is also significantly related to the strategic role of HR. It is impossible to tell from the data whether the correlations with service effectiveness mean that providing good services is a prerequisite to playing a strategic role or simply mean that HR organizations that are doing a good job at service delivery also are partners in strategy.

The results with respect to corporate roles show the lowest correlations with HR's role in strategy. Effectively working with corporate boards seems to be strongly related to being a strategic partner for both HR executives and managers, but it is the only corporate role item that is significantly correlated for both HR executives and managers.

Especially as judged by managers, effectively performing most of the HR corporate roles is not strongly associated with HR's role in strategy. This is a somewhat surprising finding, given that performing effectively in these areas often has been touted as a necessary credibility builder in order for the HR function to play a key strategic role.

HR leaders show an association between their ratings of effectiveness in operating HR centers of excellence and service centers and their ratings of their role in strategy. This association may reflect the fact that the effect of these activities on either supporting or freeing up HR to act more strategically is better understood by HR leaders than by other managers. Centers of excellence, in particular, can provide valuable strategy information and knowledge. Line managers may simply see effectiveness in these areas as sound operational management.

The Importance of HR Performance

The results on the importance of HR performance in Table 13.2 show very high ratings. The highest importance ratings for managers concern improving decisions about human capital and providing HR services. It is interesting that both HR executives and managers rate providing HR services very highly. This finding once again makes the point that HR must not lose sight of the importance of delivering basic HR services.

There is virtually no difference between HR executives and line managers. Both see HR performance as very important. There are only two items where there is a significant disagreement. HR executives attach more importance than managers to developing business strategies, while managers put more importance on decisions about human capital.

For managers, HR's developing business strategies is ranked the lowest area in importance. This result reinforces a pattern we saw earlier: that business leaders seem to value HR's contribution to decisions about human capital but do not value its developing strategies as highly; HR executives, however, see both as almost equally important. One implication of this pattern is that HR leaders may need to do some selling to the non-HR community with respect to what they can contribute to strategy.

As for the correlations between HR's role in strategy and the HR activity importance ratings, a number of items are statistically significant. The majority of the strongest relationships involve responses from HR executives. Not surprisingly, playing a major role in strategy is associated with working with the corporate board and the business and strategy items. It seems clear that in organizations where HR plays a strong role in strategy, both the HR executives and other managers see the importance of HR having been able to provide change consulting services and useful data to corporate boards. Here too, however, there is a difference between HR executives and other managers. Unlike the managers' responses, the importance that HR executives attach to their role in

Table 13.2. Importance of HR Performance

Activities	HR Executives		Managers		Importance Correlations of HR Executives with Managers
	Mean	Correlation with HR Role in Strategy	Mean	Correlation with HR Role in Strategy	
Overall Importance	**8.1**	**.28***	**8.0**	**.23^t**	**.31**
HR Services	**8.3**	**.16**	**8.4**	**.18**	**.44***
Providing HR services	9.0	.04	8.8	-.02	.03
Tailoring human resource practices to fit business needs	8.4	.05	8.5	.21^t	.25^t
Helping shape a viable employment relationship for the future	8.6	.06	8.6	.13	.39**
Being an employee advocate	7.9	.18^t	7.9	.16	.45***
Analyzing HR and business metrics	7.9	.16	8.1	.19^t	.32*
Corporate Roles	**7.6**	**.20**	**7.5**	**.23^t**	**.21**
Managing outsourcing of transactional services (e.g. benefits)	7.9	.04	7.7	.13	.24^t
Managing outsourcing of HR expertise (e.g. compensation design)	7.4	-.08	7.4	-.09	-.08
Operating HR centers of excellence	7.7	.09	7.6	.28*	.01
Operating HR shared service units	7.6	.20^t	7.4	.25*	.09
Working with the corporate board	8.0	.38***	8.0	.29*	.36**
Business and Strategy	**8.4**	**.33***	**8.2**	**.28***	**.30***
Providing change consulting services	8.2	.18^t	8.1	.19^t	.19
Being a business partner	9.0	.21*	8.7	.20^t	.06
Helping to develop business strategies	8.0	.36***	7.3[1]	.16	.38**
Improving decisions about human capital	8.3	.21*	8.8[1]	.16	.03

Scale response: 1 = not important, 10 = very important

[1] Significant difference ($p \leq .05$) between HR executives and managers.

Significance level: ^{t} $p \leq 0.10$ * $p \leq 0.05$ ** $p \leq 0.01$ *** $p \leq 0.001$

developing business strategies is related to their perception of their role in strategy.

The final column of Table 13.2 shows the correlations between the importance ratings given by HR managers and those given by managers. Unlike the effectiveness ratings, these ratings do not display a consistent pattern of high positive relationships. A number of the relationships are statistically significant, but many are not. What this suggests is that in many organizations there is little relationship between HR executives' and other managers' views of what is important.

The lack of agreement is particularly surprising when it comes to activities like operating centers of excellence and managing shared service units. These are both areas where one would think there would be significant agreement in the views of people in the same organization. The clear implication of this result is that HR executives need to work harder to make sure that there is a common understanding of HR priorities and alignment with what is expected of the HR function.

Conclusion

HR executives and other managers are apparently in general agreement about how effective HR is. It also appears that HR has improved its effectiveness since 1995. It has been particularly effective at delivering HR services. Delivering HR services is seen by HR executives as one of its most important contribution areas. The other important area, according to HR executives, is business and strategy.

HR Executives say that a strong emphasis needs to be placed on HR's role as a business partner and on improving decisions about human capital. These are areas of relatively low effectiveness for HR, and thus there is a tremendous opportunity for improvement on the part of HR. They are also areas that are related to the strategic involvement of the HR function. Thus, by making improvements in these areas, HR is likely to become much more of a strategic partner.

CHAPTER 14

Determinants of HR Effectiveness

What determines how effective an HR organization is? To answer this question, we need to look at the relationship between the effectiveness of the HR organization and the practices and activities that are likely to influence effectiveness.

Time Spent

Three aspects of how HR spends its time are related to HR executives ratings of its effectiveness, although there is little relationship for line managers. As can be seen in Table 14.1, our results show a strong negative relationship between the amount of time HR executives report their function spends maintaining records and the effectiveness of the HR organization. The relationship is also negative for managers. The other two of HR's more traditional roles—auditing/controlling and providing services—are unrelated to either group's HR effectiveness ratings. Time spent developing HR systems and practices is positively related in the eyes of HR executives, while the relationship is negative, although not significantly, for managers.

The correlation between time spent on being a strategic partner and HR effectiveness is consistent with the correlation between HR effectiveness and the role which HR plays in strategy, as reported in Chapter 13. The more HR is involved in business strategy, the more effective HR is seen to be—a relationship that is significant for HR executive ratings but does not attain significance for managers. At least from the perspective of HR executives, the function is more effective when it spends more time on business strategy.

HR Strategy

It makes a difference what kind of strategic activities HR is involved in. Table 14.2 shows the relationship between HR strategy activities and HR effectiveness. All the correlations are positive and most reach statistical significance. The strongest correlations for both HR executives and managers are between HR effectiveness and designing the organization structure to implement strategy, designing the criteria for strategic success, and deciding among the best strategy options.

Table 14.1. Relationship of HR Roles (Time Spent) and HR Effectiveness

Roles	HR Executives Rating of HR Effectiveness[1]	Manager Rating of HR Effectiveness[2]
Maintaining Records Collect, track, and maintain data on employees	-.47***	-.28[t]
Auditing/Controlling Ensure compliance to internal operations, regulations, and legal and union requirements	-.04	.04
Human Resources Service Provider Assist with implementation and administration of HR practices	-.04	.07
Development of Human Resources Systems and Practices Develop new HR systems and practices	.25[t]	-.11
Strategic Business Partner As a member of the management team, involved with strategic HR planning, organizational design, and strategic change	.29*	.18

Significance level: [t] $p \le 0.10$ * $p \le 0.05$ ** $p \le 0.01$ *** $p \le 0.001$

[1] Based on total score for all fourteen effectiveness items as rated by HR executives.

[2] Based on total score for all fourteen effectiveness items as rated by managers.

Table 14.2. Relationship of HR Strategy Activities to HR Effectiveness

Activities	HR Effectiveness	
	HR Executives[1]	Managers[2]
Help identify or design strategy options	.27[t]	.32*
Help decide among the best strategy options	.40**	.39**
Help plan the implementation of strategy	.28*	.24[t]
Help design the criteria for strategic success	.39**	.29*
Help identify new business opportunities	.23[t]	.39**
Assess the organizations readiness to implement strategies	.25[t]	.30*
Help design the organization structure to implement strategy	.38**	.38**
Assess possible merger, acquisition or divestiture strategies	.22	.25[t]
Work with the corporate board on business strategy	.27[t]	.29*
Recruit and develop talent	.29*	.37**

Significance level: [t] $p \le 0.10$ * $p \le 0.05$ ** $p \le 0.01$ *** $p \le 0.001$

[1] Based on total score for all fourteen effectiveness items as rated by HR executives.

[2] Based on total score for all fourteen effectiveness items as rated by managers.

Table 14.3. Relationship of HR Strategy Items to HR Effectiveness

	HR Effectiveness[1]
HR Strategy	**.47*****
Data-based talent strategy	.49***
Partner with line in developing business strategy	.45***
A human capital strategy that is integrated with business strategy	.46***
Provides analytic support for business decision-making	.34*
Provides HR data to support change management	.42**
HR drives change management	.42**
Makes rigorous data based decisions about human capital management	.46***

Significance level:　　　$^{t}\,p \leq 0.10$　　　$^{*}\,p \leq 0.05$　　　$^{**}\,p \leq 0.01$　　　$^{***}\,p \leq 0.001$

[1] Based on total score for all fourteen effectiveness items as rated by HR executives.

There are some areas where the HR executives' correlations differ from those of the managers. Identifying strategy options, new business opportunities, and recruiting/developing talent are more strongly related to the manager ratings of HR effectiveness than to HR executives' effectiveness ratings. In these areas, HR may be failing to recognize that in the eyes of managers their contributions are important.

The extent to which the HR function has a highly developed HR strategy and role in driving strategic change is clearly related to HR executives' ratings of HR effectiveness. Table 14.3 shows that all the relationships between the HR strategy items and effectiveness are statistically significant. The weakest relationship concerns analytics support for business decision-making; all the other items have essentially the same correlation. These results once again confirm the importance of HR's working in the areas of analysis, strategy, and organizational change. Perhaps the best overall conclusion is that HR is more effective when it plays a major role in strategy development and does not spend a large amount of time on maintaining records and HR administration.

HR Organization and Activities

The effectiveness of the HR organization is clearly related to certain aspects of how it is organized. As can be seen in Table 14.4, the use of service teams is strongly related to organizational effectiveness, as is the use of information technology. This sends a strong message to organizations about the usefulness of creating teams to provide services and of developing centers of excellence. It also validates the importance of using information technology in HR.

Table 14.4. Relationship of HR Organization to HR Effectiveness

HR Organization	HR Effectiveness[1]	
	2001	2004
HR service teams	.35***	.53***
Decentralization	.10	.02
Resource efficiency	—	.28*
Information technology	—	.59***
HR talent development	—	-.01

Significance level: [t] $p \leq 0.10$ * $p \leq 0.05$ ** $p \leq 0.01$ *** $p \leq 0.001$

[1] Based on total score for all fourteen effectiveness items as rated by HR executives.

Somewhat surprisingly, doing HR talent development is not significantly related to the effectiveness of the HR organization. It is also notable that decentralization is not correlated with HR effectiveness.

The relationship between HR activity changes and HR effectiveness is shown in Table 14.5. The results in 2004 show only one strong relationship. It is very consistent with our other findings concerning organization design and organization development. Increasing the time spent in this area is significantly associated with high levels of HR organizational effectiveness. Interestingly, increasing the amount of time spent on compensation and benefits was significantly related to HR effectiveness in 2001, but this relationship is no longer present in 2004. This suggests that the importance of time spent in various activity domains may vary depending on what is happening in the business environment.

Table 14.6, which focuses on the relationship between outsourcing and HR effectiveness, shows relatively few statistically significant relationships. The general trend is toward positive relationships, but the degree to which individual activities are outsourced clearly is not a significant predictor or cause of HR effectiveness.

It is interesting to note the negative correlation between outsourcing planning activities and HR effectiveness. This finding may reflect a few cases where it is outsourced because it is not being delivered effectively by an ineffective internal HR group. Our data show (see Table 8.1) that fewer than 10 percent of companies outsource planning, and then only partially.

Table 14.5. Relationship of HR Activity Changes to HR Effectiveness

Activities	HR Effectiveness[1]	
	2001	2004
Design and organizational development	.18[t]	.29*
Compensation and benefits	.28**	-.08
Legal and regulatory	.07	.16
Employee development	.11	.20
Recruitment and selection	.07	.13
Metrics	—	.16
HR information systems	.08	-.10
Union relations	-.06	.16

Significance level: [t] $p \leq 0.10$ * $p \leq 0.05$ ** $p \leq 0.01$ *** $p \leq 0.001$

[1] Based on total score for all fourteen effectiveness items as rated by HR executives.

Table 14.6. Relationship of Outsourcing to HR Effectiveness

Outsourcing	HR Effectiveness[1]
Overall outsourcing	.19
Planning	-.25[t]
Organizational design/development	-.09
Training	.13
HRIS and record keeping	.23[t]
Staffing and career development	.24[t]
Metrics	.17
Benefits	-.00
Compensation	.06
Legal affairs	.24[t]
Affirmative action	-.07
Employee assistance	.19
Competency/talent assessment	.26[t]
Union relations	-.15

Significance level: [t] $p \leq 0.10$ * $p \leq 0.05$ ** $p \leq 0.01$ *** $p \leq 0.001$

[1] Based on total score for all fourteen effectiveness items as rated by HR executives.

Table 14.7. Relationship of IT Use to HR Effectiveness

	Mean HR Effectiveness[1]	
Information Technology	**2001**	**2004**
Completely integrated HR IT system	**6.6**	**7.8**
Most processes are IT based but not fully integrated	**6.5**	**7.0**
Some HR processes are IT Based	**6.0**	**6.5**
Little IT present in the HR function	**4.6**	**6.5**
No IT present	**5.6**	**No respondents**

[1] Based on total score for all fourteen effectiveness items as rated by HR executives;

Scale response: 1 = not meeting needs, 10 = all needs met

Information Technology

The results from 2001 showed a clear relationship between IT use and HR effectiveness. This relationship is also present in 2004. As can be seen in Table 14.7, organizations with completely integrated systems tend to be rated the most effective. This finding is consistent with an earlier one, which showed that the HR functions using information technology for the most HR processes tend to be perceived as the most effective.

Table 14.8 looks in more depth at the uses of IT. It shows that using IT for virtually every purpose is significantly related to the effectiveness of the HR function. The only exception here is for financial transactions. Correlations are particularly strong with respect to salary planning, management tools, employee training, and personnel records.

Table 14.9 provides more detail concerning the relationship between information technology and HR effectiveness. It looks at the relationship between the effectiveness of the overall HR IT system and the overall effectiveness of HR. Here, our results show very strong positive correlations.

Metrics and Analytics

The use of HR metrics and analytics is strongly related to HR effectiveness. As can be seen in Table 14.10, the more an organization uses and has HR metrics and analytics, the more effective the HR function is. The only use that does not show a significant relationship is benchmarking analytics and measures against data from outside organizations— perhaps because benchmarking has become such a basic practice that it offers no particular unique value. All the other uses have strong, statistically significant relationships. Undoubtedly, this finding reflects the

Table 14.8. Relationship of IT System Use to HR Effectiveness

Use	HR Effectiveness[1]
Personnel records	.40**
Job information	.32*
Employee training	.40**
Management tools	.42**
Salary planning/administration	.44***
Performance management	.29*
Financial transactions	.21

Significance level: [t] $p \leq 0.10$ * $p \leq 0.05$ ** $p \leq 0.01$ *** $p \leq 0.001$

[1] Based on total score for all fourteen effectiveness items as rated by HR executives.

Table 14.9. Relationship of HR IT Effectiveness to HR Effectiveness

HR IT Outcomes	HR Effectiveness[1]
Effectiveness	.43***
Employee satisfaction	.52***
Efficiency	.64***
Business effectiveness	.48***

Significance level: [t] $p \leq 0.10$ * $p \leq 0.05$ ** $p \leq 0.01$ *** $p \leq 0.001$

[1] Based on total score for all fourteen effectiveness items as rated by HR executives.

positive advantages of measuring and analyzing HR practices and human capital.

The overall effectiveness of the HR organization is strongly related to the effectiveness of the HR metrics and analytics activities in the organization. As can be seen in Table 14.11, all of the items concerned with metrics and analytics effectiveness are strongly related to HR effectiveness. Somewhat surprisingly, there is little difference in the size of the correlations. Slightly higher correlations exist for metrics having to do with the HR department operation and HR programs, but all of the

Table 14.10. Relationship of HR Metrics and Analytics Use to HR Effectiveness

Practices	HR Effectiveness
Impact	
Collect metrics that measure the business impact of HR programs and processes?	.41**
Effectiveness	
Use dashboards or scorecards to evaluate HR's performance?	.39**
Use measures and analytics to evaluate and track the performance of outsourced HR activities?	.43***
Have metrics and analytics that reflect the effects of HR programs on the workforce (such as, competence, motivation, attitudes, behaviors, etc.)?	.30*
Have the capability to conduct cost-benefit analyses (also called utility analyses) of HR programs?	.51***
Efficiency	
Measure the financial efficiency of HR operations (e.g. cost-per-hire, time-to-fill, training costs)?	.51***
Collect metrics that measure the cost of providing HR services?	.44***
Benchmark analytics and measures against data from outside organizations (e.g., Saratoga, Mercer, Hewitt, etc.)?	.16

Significance level: ^{t} $p \le 0.10$ * $p \le 0.05$ ** $p \le 0.01$ *** $p \le 0.001$

[1] Based on total score for all fourteen effectiveness items as rated by HR executives.

activities are significantly related to the effectiveness of the HR function. This provides clear evidence that having effective HR analytics and metrics is a way to improve the effectiveness of the HR in the organization—possibly because it helps to make the HR organization more strategic and that, in turn, makes it more effective. It is also possible that even when metrics are not used to advance strategic decisions, their existence signals rigor, which is regarded as indicating HR effectiveness. Thus, perhaps at this point in the evolution of the HR profession, demonstrating effective use of metrics and analytics in virtually any HR area is a significant contributor to HR effectiveness.

The most justifiable conclusion is that the use of metrics and analytics is clearly tied to the HR effectiveness and an opportunity for greater activity. This is true for both assessing the operation of the HR function and

Table 14.11. Relationship of HR Metrics and Analytics Effectiveness to HR Effectiveness

Effectiveness	HR Effectiveness[1]
Assessing HR programs before they are implemented — not just after they are operational	.48***
Pinpointing HR programs that should be discontinued	.54***
Evaluating the effectiveness of most HR programs and practices	.54***
Assessing and improving the HR department operations	.60***
Connecting human capital practices to organizational performance	.41**
Assessing and improving the human capital strategy of the company	.52***
Identifying where talent has the greatest potential for strategic impact	.47***
Contributing to decisions about business strategy and human capital management	.52***
Supporting organizational change efforts	.44***
Making decisions and recommendations that reflect your company's competitive situation	.43***
Assessing the feasibility of new business strategies	.45***

Significance level: $^t p \leq 0.10$ $^* p \leq 0.05$ $^{**} p \leq 0.01$ $^{***} p \leq 0.001$

[1] Based on total score for all fourteen effectiveness items as rated by HR executives.

relating HR programs and practices to organizational performance. It seems particularly important that HR develop greater effectiveness in metrics and analytics areas, given the relatively low ratings that this area received when HR executives were asked to evaluate their companies' performance (see Table 11.3). The typical response was "somewhat effective" to all of these items.

Decision Science

The sophistication of managers' decision science about human capital is shown to be clearly and strongly related to HR effectiveness. As can be seen in Table 14.12, all the decision science items are highly correlated with HR effectiveness in the eyes of HR executives and line managers. The highest correlation for HR executives concerns HR leaders' identifying unique strategy insights by connecting human capital to business strategy, and business leaders' using sound principles of organization design.

It is interesting that the decision skills of business leaders are highly related to HR effectiveness. This result suggests that it takes the right

Table 14.12. Relationship of Decision Science Sophistication to HR Effectiveness

Decision-making	HR Effectiveness[1]	
	HR Executives	Managers
Business leaders' decisions that depend upon or affect human capital (e.g., layoffs, rewards, etc.) are as rigorous, logical, and strategically relevant as their decisions about resources such as money, technology, and customers	.45***	.65***
Business leaders understand and use sound principles when making decisions about:		
1. Motivation	.44***	.38**
2. Development and learning	.39**	.44***
3. Labor markets	.48***	.47***
4. Culture	.46***	.63***
5. Organizational design	.61***	.72***
6. Business strategy	.49***	.50***
HR leaders identify unique strategy insights by connecting human capital issues to business strategy	.62***	.69***
HR leaders have a good understanding about where and why human capital makes the biggest difference in their business	.53***	.61***
Business leaders have a good understanding about where and why human capital makes the biggest difference in their business	.48***	.51***

Significance level: [t] $p \leq 0.10$ * $p \leq 0.05$ ** $p \leq 0.01$ *** $p \leq 0.001$

[1] Based on total score for all fourteen effectiveness items as rated by HR executives.

Table 14.13. Relationship of HR Skill Satisfaction to HR Effectiveness

HR Skills	HR Effectiveness[1]	
	HR Executives	Managers
HR technical skills	.59***	.66***
Organizational dynamics	.63***	.79***
Business partner skills	.65***	.80***
Administrative skills	.33*	.61***
Metrics skills	.58***	.57***

Significance level: [t] $p \leq 0.10$ * $p \leq 0.05$ ** $p \leq 0.01$ *** $p \leq 0.001$

[1] Based on total score for all fourteen effectiveness items as rated by HR executives.

HR design, staffing, and activities as well as the right customers (business executives) in order for the HR function to be effective.

Skill Satisfaction

Table 14.13 shows the relationships between HR skill satisfaction and HR effectiveness. There are strong correlations for all kinds of skills, except for administrative skills. This relationship is statistically significant, but particularly in the eyes of HR executives, it is not as strong as for the other types of skills. This result once again confirms the importance of HR professionals having skills beyond just HR technical skills and administrative skills; they clearly need to have skills in organizational dynamics and effectiveness, in metrics, and as business partners.

Summary and Conclusions

Our results show a number of strong relationships between the effectiveness of the HR function and the way it is organized, managed, and staffed. Among the most important findings are the following:

- Spending time on maintaining records is negatively related to effectiveness, while being a strategic partner is positively related.

- Strategic activities such as designing an organization's criteria for strategic success and choosing strategy options are strongly related to HR effectiveness.

- Using information technology and service teams as delivery mechanisms for HR services are strongly related to HR effectiveness.

- Increased focus on organization design and development is related to HR effectiveness.

- Having a completely integrated HR IT system leads to the highest level of HR effectiveness.

- Having an IT system that is usable for salary planning, that provides management tools, that trains employees, and that maintains personnel records is related to HR effectiveness.

- The effectiveness of the HR IT system is strongly related to the overall effectiveness of the HR organization.

- Having a variety of HR metrics and analytics is strongly related to HR effectiveness.

- The effectiveness of the HR metrics systems in an organization is strongly related to HR effectiveness.

- Decision science sophistication for both managers and HR managers is strongly related to the effectiveness of the HR function.

- There is a clear relationship between the skills of HR managers and the effectiveness of the HR function.

CHAPTER 15

HR Excellence

There is no question that a consensus is emerging about what the new HR *should be*, and that HR executives are focusing on and thinking of new ways of adding value. But is the HR function changing? Our study provides the best data available to answer this question. Other studies have asked about the *importance* of new directions and skills; ours focuses on *practice* and how it has changed from 1995 to 2004.

Our study examines change by measuring the use of practices at four points in time. Other studies have asked individuals to report on the amount and kind of change that has occurred. Reports of change are generally less valid than are comparisons of data collected at two or more points in time, because the former are influenced by memory and other factors. This is demonstrated in our study by the responses to the item concerning how time is spent.

Executives responding to each of our four surveys report that there has been a significant shift during the last five to seven years in the way HR time is being spent. However, when we examine changes in practice using reports of current practice from different time periods, the percentages have not shifted. This is much better evidence about the kind and amount of change that is happening than are reports of whether change had occurred.

A comparison of the results of our 1995, 1998, 2001, and 2004 surveys establishes that some changes in the HR function have occurred, and that those changes are in the direction of HR's becoming more of a business and strategic partner. A number of significant changes have also occurred in how HR functions are organized and how they deliver services. The most important changes in HR are:

- HR is more likely to use service teams to support and service business units.

- Companies are more likely to have similar HR practices in their different business units.

- HR reports paying increasing attention to recruitment and selection and less attention to union relations. It is paying increased attention to employee development, HRIS systems, metrics, compensation, and organization design and development.

- The use of outsourcing for HRIS, benefits, compensation, and affirmative action has increased.

- More companies have integrated HR information technology.

- Employees and managers are increasingly making use of Web-enabled systems that provide job information and performance management capabilities.

- There is greater satisfaction with the organizational dynamics skills of the HR staff.

- HR is increasingly effective in helping shape a viable employment relationship for the future, providing HR services, managing outsourcing, and providing change consulting.

- The effectiveness of the HR organization has increased in a number of areas, including business and strategy, corporate roles, and services.

In comparing the 1995, 1998, and 2001 results to the 2004 results, it is clear that a number of things have not changed very much. Among them are the following:

- The amount of time spent on various human resource activities.

- The extent to which HR is a full partner in shaping business strategy.

- The rotation of individuals into, out of, and within HR.

- The use of shared services.

- The problems that occur when outsourcing.

- The use of outsourcing for organization development, employee assistance, and HR planning.

- The business partner skills of members of the HR organization.

Overall, when we compare our data from 1995, 1998, and 2001 with the 2004 results, more things stayed the same than changed. Although many of the changes we did find are significant and important, the amount of change is surprisingly small.

Frankly, given the tremendous amount of attention that has been given to the importance of HR's being more of a value-added function, becoming a business and strategic partner, and adding value in a number of new ways, we expected much more change. Somehow the HR organization has managed to maintain a relatively stable orientation, despite the amount of change that is going on around it. This finding raises a critical question: Are there particular organizational conditions that are associated with change in the HR function?

Strategic Focuses

Our study found a strong relationship between what is happening in the HR function and a company's strategic focuses. In particular, the degree to which organizations had knowledge and organizational performance strategies is related to the degree to which the HR function fit the vision of a business and strategic partner. To a lesser extent, the same was true of companies with strategies focusing on quality and speed. For example, companies that reported HR was a full partner, or had an input role to business strategy, have a greater emphasis on knowledge and information-based strategies. Generally speaking, an emphasis on knowledge, competencies, and human capital creates a much more favorable situation for the HR function because it places a premium on acquiring, developing, utilizing, and retaining talent.

One interesting theme in our results is the association of an emphasis on knowledge and competencies with the use and, to a lesser extent, the effectiveness of HR IT, and especially with providing knowledge and management tools through it. This emphasis on HR IT is compatible with current ideas about knowledge management that stress that IT is a powerful tool for making knowledge available through an organization (Davenport and Prusak, 1998). Knowledge can be embedded in tools that extend the knowledge workers' capabilities (Leonard-Barton, 1995)—not only the tools that are offered to employees and managers in general but also the tools that are used by HR.

Knowledge and competency emphases are also associated with the more interpersonal aspects of HR, such as the use of service teams and organizational dynamics skills. This association fits with current understandings that IT is insufficient for delivering knowledge, because the application of knowledge to solve complex and uncertain problems often requires interpersonal exchange in which people with various knowledge bases work together (Mohrman, Finegold, and Klein, 2002).

Strategies and initiatives that focus on performance capabilities relate to many of the same features of the HR organization as knowledge and competency emphases. In fact, all six of the strategy focuses are associated with greater use of service teams, the extent to which a talent strategy is in place, the emphasis on employee development, and the effectiveness of HR IT in improving business performance. Thus, it appears that the most potent combination of company strategies that drives change in HR is a focus on knowledge, combined with a focus on organizational performance.

Overall, our results clearly show that strategy initiatives do make a difference in the way the HR function operates and in its ability to be a

Creating a Strategic Human Resources Organization

successful business partner. When there is an explicit focus on knowledge and organizational performance capabilities, HR performs more high-value-added activities, and the HR function is more positively regarded. To a lesser extent, quality- and information-based strategies demonstrate the same relationship. Organizational strategies that entail growth and restructuring the organization in most cases do not relate to the way the HR function operates.

HR Effectiveness

The factors leading to HR effectiveness are a combination of approaches that promote efficiency in routine transactional processing and allow HR professionals to focus on expanding their knowledge base, providing expertise, and partnering with others in the business. In Chapter 14 we gave a long list of practices that are associated with effectiveness; the list represents an actionable agenda for most HR functions. It is also marked by another characteristic: most of these practices are not widely used, and there was little increase in their use between our survey in 1995 and our survey in 2004. This strongly suggests that one reason why HR is not increasing in effectiveness is that it has failed to do the things that it needs to do in order to be perceived as more effective.

HR as a Strategic Partner

The data concerning what determines the effectiveness of the HR organization are clearly consistent with the argument that HR can and should be more of a strategic partner. However, HR is not a strategic partner in most organizations. It appears to have some influence in the areas of staffing and strategy, and some influence with respect to organizational structure issues and implementing strategy. Nevertheless, it seems to be a weak player when it comes to the development of strategy, consideration of strategic options, and other strategy areas including acquisitions and mergers.

A number of factors are clearly related to HR's being a strategic partner:

- Using information technology
- Focusing on HR talent development
- Using HR service teams
- Focusing HR activities more on organization design, organization development, employee development, and metrics
- Using IT systems for training and development
- Having an effective HR IT system
- Having effective HR metrics and analytics

Exhibit 15.1. Factors Associated with HR as a Strategic Partner

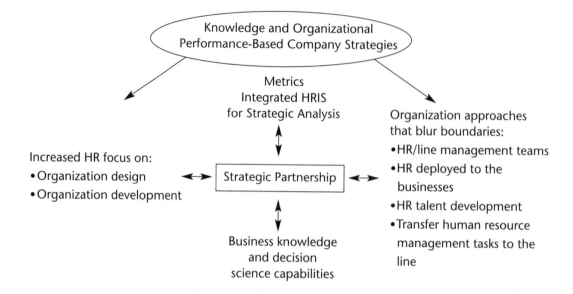

- Having business leaders who make rigorous, logical human capital decisions

- Having an HR staff with technical, organizational dynamics, business partner, and metrics skills

- Providing effective services, fulfilling its corporate roles, and effectively supporting business strategy

In general, the strategic partnership model developed by Lawler and Mohrman (2003b) based on our 2001 survey is supported by the results of the 2004 survey. An updated version of it is presented in Exhibit 15.1. Overall, it shows that being a business partner demands HR's having high levels of knowledge and skill, and making use of organization designs and practices that link HR managers to business units.

Obstacles to Change

Why hasn't HR changed more? There are a number of plausible explanations. One is that there may not have been enough pressure to change. The existing role and activities of HR may be well institutionalized in a kind of co-dependency relationship. The individuals in the HR function are satisfied with their current role and comfortable delivering services in a traditional mode; at the same time, the recipients of these services, who are also satisfied with an administrative function that removes "onerous" HR responsibilities from the line, are not asking for change. This situation leads to an institutionalized devaluation of the

Creating a Strategic Human Resources Organization

HR function by the line because of its low level of contribution to the business, but also to an unwillingness to let HR change, because it serves them.

In addition, the "war for talent" of the 1990s may, ironically, have operated against the upgrading of the HR function. It may have focused a disproportionate amount of professional HR time on delivering services related to recruiting, orienting, developing, and retaining employees, leaving HR little time and few resources to spend on upgrading its competencies and systems and being a strategic partner. HR time and attention may have been sidetracked by bidding wars for talented employees and by the need to generate and administer reward systems that matched the market that existed during the high-technology boom period.

There is a certain service imperative that is associated with recruiting, developing, motivating, and retaining employees that locks most HR professionals into patterns of activity that are difficult to change. Our finding that the amount of attention being paid to almost all HR activities has increased would seem to support the view that even though there is an emerging consensus about what constitutes high-value-added HR activities, HR functions still find themselves having to spend more time on activities that they know to be low in business value.

Low skill levels in the HR function offer an additional explanation for the limited change in the HR function. Just how difficult it is to change the HR function becomes apparent when we look at the kinds of skills that members of the HR function must have in order to be rated highly and to play the strategic and business partner roles. They need a broad range of skills ranging from relatively routine administrative processing skills to organizational dynamics and business partner skills. Although business partner and organizational dynamics skills are most highly related to effectiveness, the HR function cannot afford to carry out their core administrative functions ineffectively. Interestingly, HR did not score very highly in administrative skills, especially with respect to managing contractors and managing IT. These are relatively new competencies that have become important with the transition to HR IT.

Business and strategic partnering effectiveness requires knowledge and skills in such areas as change management, strategic planning, and organizational design. It also requires a decision science for human capital that provides logical and unique strategic insights by using human capital principles (Boudreau and Ramstad, 2005b). These areas involve complex judgments, and HR professionals have traditionally had little experience with them. Such expertise is both hard to acquire and in short supply. Becoming expert in business partnering demands the acquisition of not only explicit knowledge but also tacit knowledge that comes from experience. Applying this expertise demands the ability to influence line management and to be part of effective teaming relationships with others who carry deep knowledge about the business and the market (Mohrman, Finegold, and Klein, 2002).

The results of our study show that although HR professionals are seen as having increased some of their business partner skills since 1995, they are still perceived to fall short in strategic planning, metrics, and cross-functional experience. Understanding the business is just a ticket to get to the table. Expertise in the other areas is required to add value once at the table. Thus, HR is in a bit of a catch-22 situation. It must get to the table and gain experience in order to gain the knowledge and skills it needs to get there!

Enabling Change

In part, the failure of HR to become a strategic partner may be because HR has not yet found a way to deliver high quality administrative services without devoting a large amount of resources to doing so. Here, our results show that HR IT offers considerable untapped potential. We did find that more HR activities are being done by employees on computer systems, potentially freeing up HR managers to do more strategic work. We also found that the effectiveness of HR IT systems in performing HR processes and enabling employee self-service was positively related to how skilled HR was seen to be in providing administrative support. The most positive outcomes of HR IT systems to date are the efficiency benefits they produce. The extent of completeness and integration of these systems is related to overall HR effectiveness.

Overall, our results suggest that an investment in a high quality HR IT system should increase the HR function's credibility and perceived value added, while decreasing the time the function spends on administrative tasks. We found some evidence of a substitution effect: providing high quality systems for administrative processing related not only to perceived administrative effectiveness but also to perceived effectiveness in all areas. This may be so because a high quality HR IT system allows the function to spend more time on developing valuable new skills. Furthermore, by offering knowledge and tools to managers and employees, a high quality HR IT system can provide new employee- and business-related services.

At this point, HR executives do not perceive computer systems to be particularly effective. They are given relatively high marks on improving HR services and speeding up HR processes but are not rated highly in most other areas. Without question, the potential exists for such systems to be a key delivery vehicle and to help make the HR organization much more effective and much more of a business partner. In particular, the value of such systems in imparting needed knowledge to managers and employees represents a growth opportunity.

To summarize, the HR function is changing, and is changing in the right direction, but change has been slow and is not taking place in all the areas where it is needed. Currently, the HR function is a long way from being a high value added strategic and business partner that delivers high quality transactional services in a cost effective manner.

For the HR function to achieve its vision of becoming a value-adding business and strategic partner, it will have to develop new skills and new tools. Additionally, it will have to organize to better deploy its resources to support a redefined role. It needs to greatly increase the exposure of HR professionals to business issues, and employ work structures that bring them together in partnership with the line and other functions. In short, as will be discussed next, it will have to move out of its comfort zone and model the processes required for the development and motivation of human capital in knowledge work firms.

Future Directions

What does the future hold for the human resources function? When we reported on the 1998 results, we said, "Change has just begun. The next decade will probably see dramatic change in the human resource function in most companies. The opportunity exists for human resource management to become a true strategic partner, and to help decide how organizations will be managed, what human resource systems will look like, and how human resource services will be created and delivered."

Our 2004 results suggest that many of the changes we predicted have not taken place. Yes, there has been change, but it is not the kind of substantial change that we thought would happen. Fortunately for our credibility as prognosticators, we are only in the middle of the new decade and still at the beginning of the new millennium. There is still quite a bit of time for HR to change dramatically in many important ways.

If anything, we feel more strongly than ever today about the importance of change in the HR organization. Organizations in the United States and the developed world have ever-higher percentages of their employees doing knowledge work. Human capital is becoming increasingly important as a source of competitive advantage, as is intellectual capital. Our study clearly shows that when organizations focus on developing their competencies, capabilities, and knowledge assets, especially when it is in combination with a strong focus on the performance capabilities of the firm, they make HR much more of a strategic and business partner, and they make changes in the HR function. Thus, there are good reasons to believe that HR will change.

How should HR be managed and structured in large corporations? Will it still be a large function, employing approximately one out of every hundred employees, and organized around its major activities, such as compensation, training, and staffing? There is good reason to believe that it will not. HR needs to look at itself much more as a business, because that is the way senior executives are beginning to look at it. It will be assessed and should assess itself according to whether it adds enough value to justify its costs.

HR as a High Value Contributor

As a business, HR potentially can have three product lines. The first is to provide the basic HR administrative services and tasks that are involved in compensating individuals, hiring them, training them, and staffing positions in the organization. The second role is as a business partner that helps business units and general managers realize their business plans. In this role, HR needs to provide advice and services concerning organizational development, change management, and the articulation between human resource management systems and business operations. This role entails leading the development and installation of human resource management practices that position the organization to execute its business plans.

The third role is to contribute to the strategic direction of the organization. It requires leading the development and assessment of the human capital and organizational capabilities required to support the long-term success of the organization. This role requires individuals who understand business strategy and how it relates to organizational capabilities and core competencies. Let us look separately at how each of these product lines within HR might develop in the future.

The administrative and functional human resource management services of an organization are clearly moving more and more toward being a commodity or product that can be delivered in a number of different ways. Historically, they have been delivered by an in-house HR function in a labor-intensive, poorly integrated, and costly manner. There is little doubt that this labor-intensive approach is obsolete and needs to be replaced by a new model. The obvious technology to replace it is an IT-based HR system that provides self-service. Today at least three models are emerging as ways to acquire the information technology needed to deliver HR services.

The first is custom systems that are designed by firms for their own use. This model is currently being used by information technology compa-

Creating a Strategic Human Resources Organization

nies such as Dell, Cisco, Hewlett-Packard, and Microsoft. Some of these systems are very impressive, allowing individuals on a self-service basis to perform a number of important HR tasks and access a great deal of information. However, it is highly unlikely that most companies will ever develop the kind of custom systems that have been developed by technology companies; doing so is simply too expensive and time consuming.

What companies can do, however, is adopt either of two other alternatives: they can buy the integrated, Web-based systems that are sold by the major ERP vendors, Oracle and SAP, or they can purchase individual HR IT applications designed to do compensation administration, staffing, training, and other HR activities from software vendors. Some good software programs exist, and when combined can produce an effective HR system for companies. However, there is a significant disadvantage associated with choosing a set of best-of-breed software systems. Making the best use of HR data often involves using them in multiple processes. In order to do so, software integration needs to occur. This can be costly and time consuming; thus, in the future, organizations will be increasingly likely to buy integrated HR systems rather than individual solutions.

A third option is complete business process outsourcing. A number of major corporations have signed contracts to outsource all of the administrative aspects of their human resource management process. Case studies of four early adopters show it resulting in significant cost savings as well as enabling some movement toward HR's becoming more of a strategic partner (Lawler, Ulrich, Fitz-enz, and Madden, 2004).

It is unlikely that any one of these three alternatives will be dominant by the end of the decade. However, it is quite likely that the majority of large firms will have highly developed, computer-based HR systems, because such systems create the opportunity to build an HR function that is not only more cost effective but also delivers a superior product. In short, they may represent a better business model than the traditional HR model when it comes to delivering routine human resource management services and administration.

Business Partner

But what about the business partner activities of HR? Can they be outsourced? Should they be outsourced? Can they be put on the Web? Should they be put on the Web? There is little doubt that some business partner activities can be greatly facilitated by the use of vendors and by the use of the Web. Effective computer systems can collect and analyze data about the condition of the human resources of an organization that have previously not been available because of the great amount of time required to collect, aggregate, and analyze such data. HR IT systems can aid in change management, business plan implementation, and the operation of the business, because they can make information readily available to employees and can easily solicit employee feedback and suggestions. In all these areas, it should be pointed out that computer systems are merely enablers; they cannot take the place of human judgment in problem-solving and decision-making that entail judgment and values.

With regard to outsourcing, many consultants can provide insight into the implementation of business plans and change management. However, our view is that organizations will always need to have skilled HR professionals to provide many of the services and the information and knowledge that are necessary in order for HR to be an effective business partner.

Performing the business partner role entails solving problems and making decisions that are value-laden, highly uncertain, and context-specific; they require an understanding of the business, its strategy, the nature of the workforce, and the required competencies. It entails the application of tacit experience-based knowledge as well as knowledge of an explicit discipline and the ability to combine HR knowledge with the perspectives of other disciplines such as business management, marketing, information technology, and technology.

The key question here is not whether professional HR executives will perform the business partner role, but whether the individuals who are currently human resource executives can perform it effectively. The evidence in this study suggests that the comfort level of human resource professionals is highest with traditional activities and modes of delivery, because it is where their effectiveness and skills are the highest. If they want to be effective business partners, they need to change their skill set and become comfortable with a variety of new activities.

HR executives need to understand and be able to formulate a business model for the HR function and to contribute to the firm's business model. They need to understand business operations better and be able to craft human resource management approaches that fit its requirements. They need to understand organization and work design and change management principles and approaches, and be able to play a leadership role when these issues are considered. They need to understand different models of staffing, compensation, and other human resources practices so that they can effectively implement HR systems that support the business plans of the organization. Finally, they need to identify the vital pivot points in the business that drive strategic and organizational effectiveness, and then connect human capital decisions to those pivot points.

Creating a Strategic Human Resources Organization

Strategic Partner

Last but certainly not least are the strategic partner activities of HR. As organizations do more knowledge work and human capital has become more important, there is no question that these activities have become more important. The rapid rate of change, the need to develop new strategies and to quickly translate them into human resource strategies, and the likelihood that the availability of talent will be a key strategic differentiator have greatly increased the importance of HR's being a strategic partner. Our view is that this can only be done by individuals who have a good understanding of business strategy, as well as of HR strategy. Some of the work that is involved in being a strategic partner can be outsourced to HR strategy vendors; however, we believe there needs to be a strong internal presence of individuals who have good HR knowledge, who can manage vendors, and who can be truly present at the table when strategy formulation and implementation is discussed by senior executives.

HR's strategic partner seat at the table needs to be filled by a senior executive in the corporation, not by a consultant. The importance of the strategic partner role, and the need to fill it with somebody who understands business, may be why almost a quarter of all chief HR executives come from the business rather than from the HR function. In essence, some companies may have decided that the HR strategic partner role is too important to leave to someone with an HR background. However, we believe that assigning the strategic role to those outside the HR profession is no substitute for developing HR executives who are experts in HR practices and principles and how those practices and principles affect the business and enable its strategy.

In the future there are likely to be great opportunities for senior HR managers to be strategic partners. Having data available from HR IT systems is one of several enablers that can strengthen their position as strategic partners. HR IT systems can, for example, help them make significant contributions to strategy formulation, by providing both cost and organizational effectiveness data with respect to human resource practices. They can provide information about how to develop certain key competencies in the workforce and about the existing levels of organizational effectiveness and organizational capabilities. These are all critical inputs to the strategic planning process. They also can enable HR executives to translate what they know about the existing organization and its capabilities into change programs, thus allowing the organization to develop the necessary capabilities to implement new strategic plans and new directions (Lawler and Worley, 2006).

The key question with respect to the strategic partner role concerns not so much whether it is an important role at this point, but how it can be filled. As with the business partner role, there is a serious question as to whether many of the current individuals in the HR function are in a position to fill it. To be specific, it is not clear whether they understand the business well enough to be a strategic partner. Many of them have never worked outside of HR and, as a result, have a limited understanding of what the business is about and what the strategic options are both with respect to business strategy and HR strategy. Moreover, the HR profession has yet to develop a decision science akin to those of marketing and finance.

HR Organization Design

A clear organizational model for the HR function seems to be emerging for companies with multiple business units. It involves creating HR leaders who partner with line management in business units. This role involves HR's contributing to business unit plans and helping to develop organizational capabilities and implement the human resource practices and people development approaches that are needed to create a competent workforce. These HR leaders are also expected to represent the central HR organization in its dealings with the business unit.

Instead of locating many of the HR services in the business unit, multibusiness corporations are creating shared-service units and corporate centers of excellence for the business units to draw on. Alternatively, they are outsourcing HR transactional services and telling the business units to use them. The role of the generalist is thus to be both a business partner and a coordinator of HR services to the business unit in which he or she works.

In essence, the HR organization appears to be becoming a type of frontback organization, with the generalist as the front, customer-focused, part. The generalist represents the HR organization in the business unit and is responsible for coordinating and delivering services from the back of the organization. The back, in this case, is the shared-services units and centers of excellence that are available to the business units, and also the services that are delivered by an HR IT system.

Looking Ahead

The opportunity for the human resource function to add value at the strategic level is great, but at the present time it is more promise than reality. For promise to become reality, HR executives need to develop new skills and knowledge, and, of course, HR needs to be able to execute human resource management and administration activities effectively. Doing the basics well is the platform upon which the HR organization needs to build its role as a strategic partner. Doing so is critical, because it demonstrates the capacity of the HR function to operate effectively as a business, and it potentially can provide the information which enables HR to be an effective strategic partner.

The need for a new business model for HR has been articulated, but the human resource function still appears to be at the very beginning of the changes that are needed in order for it to become reality. Our study demonstrates that the change process is slower than anticipated, but it has identified a clear agenda of actions that can yield an HR function capable of adding more value to the business. We still believe there will be enormous change in the design and operation of human resource functions in this decade. We have said it before and we say it again: the HR function needs to look seriously at how it can reinvent itself. The old approaches and models are simply not good enough.

REFERENCES   Becker, B. E., and Huselid, M. A. 1998. "High Performance Work Systems and Firm Performance: A Synthesis of Research and Managerial Implications." *Research in Personnel and Human Resources Management*, 16, 53–101.

BNA. 2001. *Human Resource Activities, Budgets and Staffs.* Washington, D.C.: BNA.

Boudreau, J. W., and Ramstad, P. M. 1997. "Measuring Intellectual Capital: Learning from Financial History." *Human Resource Management*, 36 (3), 343–56.

Boudreau, J. W., and Ramstad, P. M. 2003. "Strategic HRM Measurement in the 21st Century: From Justifying HR to Strategic Talent Leadership." In M. Goldsmith, R. P. Gandossy, and M. S. Efron (eds.), *HRM in the 21st Century*, 79–90. New York: John Wiley.

Boudreau, J. W., and Ramstad, P. M. 2005a. "Talentship and the Evolution of Human Resource Management: From 'Professional Practices' to 'Strategic Talent Decision Science.'" *Human Resource Planning Journal*, 28 (2), 17–26.

Boudreau, J. W., and Ramstad, P. M. 2005b. "Talentship, Talent Segmentation, and Sustainability: A New HR Decision Science Paradigm for a New Strategy Definition." In M. Losey, S. Meisinger, and D. Ulrich (eds.), *The Future of Human Resources Management*. Washington, D.C.: Society for Human Resource Management.

Boudreau, J. W., and Ramstad, P. M. 2005c. "Where's Your Pivotal Talent?" *Harvard Business Review*. April, 83 (4), 23–24.

Boudreau, J. W., and Ramstad, P. M. (2006). "Talentship and Human Resource Measurement and Analysis: From ROI to Strategic Organizational Change." *Human Resource Planning Journal*.

Brockbank, W. 1999. "If HR Were Really Strategically Proactive: Present and Future Directions in HR's Contribution to Competitive Advantage." *Human Resource Management*, 38, 337–52.

Brockbank, W., and Ulrich, D. 2003. *Competencies for the New HR.* Washington, D.C.: University of Michigan Business School, Society for Human Resource Management and Global Consulting Alliance.

Cascio, W. 2000. *Costing Human Resources.* 4th ed. Cincinnati: South-Western.

Csoka, L. S. 1995. *Rethinking Human Resources.* Report no. 1124-95. New York: Conference Board.

Csoka, L. S., and Hackett, B. 1998. *Transforming the HR Function for Global Business Success.* New York: Conference Board.

Davenport, T. H., and Prusak, L. 1998. *Working Knowledge: How Organizations Manage What They Know.* Boston: Harvard Business School.

Eichinger, B., and Ulrich, D. 1995. "Human Resources Challenges: Today and Tomorrow." In *The First Annual State-of-the-Art Council Report from the Human Resource Planning Society.* New York: Human Resource Planning Society.

Galbraith, J. R. 2002. *Designing Organizations.* San Francisco: Jossey-Bass.

Gates, S. 2004. *Measuring More than Efficiency.* Research Report no. R-1356-04-RR. New York: Conference Board.

Gubman, E. 2004. "HR Strategy and Planning: From Birth to Business Results." *Human Resource Planning,* 27 (1), 13–23.

Lawler, E. E. 1995. "Strategic Human Resources Management: An Idea Whose Time Has Come." In B. Downie and M. L. Coates (eds.), *Managing Human Resources in the 1990s and Beyond: Is the Workplace Being Transformed?,* 46–70. Kingston, Ontario: IRC Press.

Lawler, E. E., Levenson, A., and Boudreau, J. W. 2004. "HR Metrics and Analytics—Uses and Impacts." *Human Resource Planning,* 27 (4), 27–35.

Lawler, E. E., and Mohrman, S. A. 2000. *Creating a Strategic Human Resources Organization.* Los Angeles: Center for Effective Organizations.

Lawler, E. E., and Mohrman, S. A. 2003a. *Creating a Strategic Human Resources Organization: An Assessment of Trends and New Directions.* Stanford: Stanford University Press.

Lawler, E. E., and Mohrman, S. A. 2003b. "HR as a Strategic Partner: What Does It Take to Make It Happen?" *Human Resource Planning,* 26 (5), 15.

Lawler, E. E., Mohrman, S. A., and Benson, G. S. 2001. *Organizing for High Performance: The CEO Report on Employee Involvement, TQM, Reengineering, and Knowledge Management in Fortune 1,000 Companies.* San Francisco: Jossey-Bass.

Lawler, E. E., Ulrich, D., Fitz-enz, J., and Madden, J. 2004. *Human Resources Business Process Outsourcing*. San Francisco: Jossey-Bass.

Lawler, E. E., and Worley, C. 2006. *Built to Change*. San Francisco: Jossey-Bass.

Leonard-Barton, D. 1995. *Wellsprings of Knowledge: Building and Sustaining the Sources of Innovation*. Boston: Harvard Business School Press.

Lev, B. 2001. *Intangibles: Management, Measurement, and Reporting*. Washington, D.C.: Brookings.

Mohrman, S. A., Cohen, S. G., and Mohrman, A. M., Jr. 1995. *Designing Team Based Organizations*. San Francisco: Jossey-Bass.

Mohrman, S. A., Finegold, D., and Klein, J. 2002. "Designing the Knowledge Enterprise: Beyond Programs and Tools." *Organization Dynamics*, 31 (2), 134–50.

Mohrman, A. M., Galbraith, J. R., Lawler, E. E., and associates. 1998. *Tomorrow's Organization: Crafting Winning Capabilities in a Dynamic World*. San Francisco: Jossey-Bass.

Mohrman, S. A., Lawler, E. E., and McMahan, G. C. 1996. *New Directions for the Human Resources Organization*. Los Angeles: Center for Effective Organizations.

Nadler, D. A., Gerstein, M. S., and Shaw, R. B. 1992. *Organizational Architecture: Designs for Changing Organizations*. San Francisco: Jossey-Bass.

SHRM (Society for Human Resource Management). 1998. *Human Resources Management*. 1998 SHRM/CCH Study. Chicago: CCH.

Smith, L. H., and Riley, C. F. 1994. *Human Resources Alignment Study, Best Practices Report: Achieving Success Through People*. Houston: American Productivity and Quality Center.

Ulrich, D. 1997. *Human Resources Champions*. Boston: Harvard Business School Press.

Ulrich, D., and Brockbank, W. 2005. *The HR Value Proposition.* Boston: Harvard Business School Press.

Ulrich, D., Losey, M. R., and Lake, G. (eds.). 1997. *Tomorrow's HR Management*. New York: Wiley.

Waterman, R. 1982. "The Seven Elements of Strategic Fit." *Journal of Business Strategy* (Winter), 69–73.

APPENDIXES

The Practice of Human Resource Management:
A Survey of the Changing Human Resource Function
Item Report (N = 100)

QUESTIONS ABOUT YOUR COMPANY AND THE HR ORGANIZATION.

	MEAN
1. How many employees are in your company?	**30,700**
2. How many full-time-equivalent employees (FTE's, exempt and non-exempt) are part of the HR function? (this number should include both centralized and decentralized staff)	**307**
3. Of the professional/managerial employees in HR, what percentage are in roles that directly support a business unit (e.g., generalists)?	**48.2%**
4. Of your professional/managerial HR employees, what percent are centralized (e.g., corporate staff)?	**38.4%**

5. What is the background of the current head of HR? (please check one response)

		MEAN
	1. Human Resource Management	**77.9%**
	2. Other Function(s), (which one(s)?_____)	**22.1%**

	MEAN
6. What percentage of your company's revenue comes from outside the United States? (if your response is 0%, skip to question 9)	**26.3%**
7. What percentage of your company's employees are located outside of the United States?	**30.5%**
8. What percentage of your company's HR professional employees are located outside the United States?	**24.1%**

	Yes	No
9. Is there a union presence in your company?	**58.9%**	**41.1%**

	MEAN
a. If yes, what percentage of your workforce is union represented	**23.2%**

10. Which of the following best describes your company? (please check one response):

		MEAN
	1. Single integrated business	**22.4%**
	2. Multiple related businesses with corporate functions providing some integrative support.	**53.1%**
	3. Several sectors or groups of business units with some corporate functions and support.	**21.4%**
	4. Multiple unrelated businesses managed independently in a "holding company" fashion.	**1.0%**
	5. Other (please specify) _____	**2.0%**

THIS SECTION ASKS QUESTIONS ABOUT STRATEGIC INITIATIVES IN YOUR COMPANY.

11. **To what extent is each of the following strategic initiatives present in your organization?**

(1 = Little or No Extent, 2 = Some Extent, 3 = Moderate Extent, *4 = Great Extent, 5 = Very Great Extent)*	Little or No Extent	Some Extent	Moderate Extent	Great Extent	Very Great Extent	MEAN
a. Building a global presence	29.3	13.1	19.2	14.1	24.2	**2.91**
b. Partnering/networking with other companies	17.0	29.0	26.0	19.0	9.0	**2.74**
c. Quality	2.0	6.0	15.0	37.0	40.0	**4.07**
d. Cycle time reduction	9.0	15.0	23.0	39.0	14.0	**3.34**
e. Accelerating new product innovation	10.0	14.0	29.0	25.0	22.0	**3.35**
f. Acquisitions	19.2	19.2	25.3	22.2	14.1	**2.93**
g. Process automation/Information technology	1.0	8.0	31.0	40.0	20.0	**3.70**
h. Customer focus	0	3.0	14.1	21.2	61.6	**4.41**
i. Technology leadership	7.1	11.1	33.3	29.3	19.2	**3.42**
j. Reducing the number of businesses you are in	56.0	23.0	14.0	6.0	1.0	**1.73**
k. Talent – being an Employer of Choice	6.0	11.0	18.0	40.0	25.0	**3.67**
l. e-Business	24.0	24.0	25.0	21.0	6.0	**2.61**
m. Cost leadership	8.0	15.0	28.0	33.0	16.0	**3.34**
n. Expansion into new markets	6.0	24.0	26.0	34.0	10.0	**3.18**
o. Exiting businesses	44.0	30.0	13.0	9.0	4.0	**1.99**
p. Human capital strategy for competitive advantage	9.0	12.0	31.0	33.0	15.0	**3.33**
q. Total Quality Management/Six Sigma	24.0	28.0	18.0	11.0	19.0	**2.73**
r. Employee involvement	4.0	22.0	25.0	35.0	14.0	**3.33**
s. Knowledge/intellectual capital management	8.0	21.0	35.0	25.0	11.0	**3.10**

QUESTIONS ABOUT THE HUMAN RESOURCE FUNCTION IN YOUR COMPANY.

12. **For each of the following HR roles, please estimate the percentage of time your HR function spends performing these roles. Please split 100% among the following categories:**

PERCENTAGES SHOULD ADD TO 100% FOR EACH COLUMN:	CURRENTLY	5-7 YEARS AGO
a. **Maintaining Records** (Collect, track and maintain data on employees)	**13.2%**	**25.9%**
b. **Auditing/Controlling** (Insure compliance to internal operations, regulations, legal and union requirements)	**13.3%**	**14.8%**
c. **Providing Human Resource Services** (Assist with implementation and administration of HR practices)	**32.0%**	**36.4%**
d. **Developing Human Resource Systems and Practices** (Develop new HR systems and practices)	**18.1%**	**12.6%**
e. **Strategic Business Partnering** (Member of the management team. Involved with strategic HR planning, organization design, and strategic change)	**23.5%**	**9.6%**
TOTAL	**100%**	**100%**

13. Which of the following best describes the relationship between the Human Resource function and the business strategy of your corporation? (please check one response)

1. Human Resource plays no role in business strategy **(GO TO QUESTION 14)**. **2.0%**

2. Human Resource is involved in implementing the business strategy. **12.2%**

3. Human Resource provides input to the business strategy and helps implement it once it has been developed **45.9%**

4. Human Resource is a full partner in developing and implementing the business strategy......**39.8%**

ANSWER QUESTIONS 13a, ONLY IF YOU CHECKED 2, 3, OR 4 FOR QUESTION 13 above.

13a. Please respond to the following questions by circling one number in each row. With respect to strategy, to what extent does the HR function ...

(1 = Little or No Extent, 2 = Some Extent, 3 = Moderate Extent, 4 = Great Extent, 5 = Very Great Extent)	Little or No Extent	Some Extent	Moderate Extent	Great Extent	Very Great Extent	MEAN
a. Help identify or design strategy options	11.5	26.0	32.3	22.9	7.3	**2.89**
b. Help decide among the best strategy options...........	7.2	23.7	35.1	28.9	5.2	**3.01**
c. Help plan the implementation of strategy..................	2.1	10.3	24.7	48.5	14.4	**3.63**
d. Help design the criteria for strategic success	8.2	16.5	35.1	30.9	9.3	**3.16**
e. Help identify new business opportunities.................	34.0	39.2	20.6	2.1	4.1	**2.03**
f. Assess the organizations readiness to implement strategies...	1.0	19.6	27.8	34.0	17.5	**3.47**
g. Help design the organization structure to implement strategy...	2.1	9.3	26.8	32.0	29.9	**3.78**
h. Assess possible merger, acquisition or divestiture strategies...	19.6	17.5	29.9	23.7	9.3	**2.86**
i. Work with the corporate board on business strategy..	28.1	22.9	22.9	17.7	8.3	**2.55**
j. Recruit and develop talent...	0	2.1	4.1	27.8	66.0	**4.58**

14. Your Company's HR Strategy

A. To what extent do each of the following describe the way your HR organization currently operates?
(1 = Little or No Extent, 2 = Some Extent, 3 = Moderate Extent, 4 = Great Extent, 5 = Very Great Extent)

B. To what extent is each a part of your organization's HR strategy for the future?
(1 = Not in our Plans, 2 = Possible Focus, 3 = An Important Future Focus)

	A. To what extent do each of the following describe the way your HR organization currently operates?						B. To what extent is each a part of your organization's HR strategy for the future?			
	Little or No Extent	Some Extent	Moderate Extent	Great Extent	Very Great Extent	MEAN	Not in our Plans	Possible Focus	An Important Future Focus	MEAN
1. Administrative processing is centralized in shared services units	4.0	11.1	21.2	39.4	24.2	**3.69**	8.4	27.4	64.2	**2.56**
2. Transactional HR work is outsourced	23.2	32.3	21.2	14.1	9.1	**2.54**	16.7	44.8	38.5	**2.22**
3. Centers of excellence provide specialized expertise	9.1	21.2	20.2	26.3	23.2	**3.33**	6.3	26.0	67.7	**2.61**
4. Decentralized HR generalists support business units	8.1	6.1	12.1	36.4	37.4	**3.89**	15.5	17.5	67.0	**2.52**
5. HR teams provide service and support the business	5.1	7.1	19.2	44.4	24.2	**3.76**	8.2	25.8	66.0	**2.58**
6. People rotate within HR	12.1	30.3	32.3	16.2	9.1	**2.80**	10.2	48.0	41.8	**2.32**
7. People rotate into HR	45.5	36.4	12.1	4.0	2.0	**1.81**	32.6	47.4	20.0	**1.87**
8. People rotate out of HR to other functions	39.2	37.1	17.5	3.1	3.1	**1.94**	27.4	54.7	17.9	**1.91**
9. Hire from the outside for senior HR positions	19.2	19.2	28.3	22.2	11.1	**2.87**	26.8	55.7	17.5	**1.91**
10. Self-funding requirements exist for HR services	39.8	25.5	20.4	10.2	4.1	**2.13**	46.8	40.4	12.8	**1.66**
11. HR systems and policies are developed through joint line/HR task teams	7.1	20.2	24.2	36.4	12.1	**3.26**	7.4	42.1	50.5	**2.43**
12. HR practices vary across business units	25.5	34.7	27.6	11.2	1.0	**2.28**	44.7	37.2	18.1	**1.73**
13. Very small corporate staff - most HR managers and professionals are out in businesses	14.3	28.6	26.5	19.4	11.2	**2.85**	26.1	39.1	34.8	**2.09**
14. Some activities that used to be done by HR are now done by line managers	10.2	31.6	33.7	19.4	5.1	**2.78**	7.4	37.2	55.3	**2.48**

Appendixes

14. Your Company's HR Strategy

A. To what extent do each of the following describe the way your HR organization currently operates?
(1 = Little or No Extent, 2 = Some Extent, 3 = Moderate Extent, 4 = Great Extent, 5 = Very Great Extent)

B. To what extent is each a part of your organization's HR strategy for the future?
(1 = Not in our Plans, 2 = Possible Focus, 3 = An Important Future Focus)

	A. To what extent do each of the following describe the way your HR organization currently operates?						B. To what extent is each a part of your organization's HR strategy for the future?			
	Little or No Extent	Some Extent	Moderate Extent	Great Extent	Very Great Extent	MEAN	Not in our Plans	Possible Focus	An Important Future Focus	MEAN
15. Some transactional activities that used to be done by HR are done by employees on a self-service basis	14.4	23.7	28.9	19.6	13.4	**2.94**	1.1	13.8	85.1	**2.84**
16. Efficient and accurate HRIS	8.2	14.3	32.7	32.7	12.2	**3.27**	0	10.6	89.4	**2.89**
17. Data automatically gathered for tracking effectiveness of HR Programs	30.6	27.6	25.5	15.3	1.0	**2.29**	3.2	41.5	55.3	**2.52**
18. HR "advice" is available on-line for managers and employees	22.4	35.7	23.5	9.2	9.2	**2.47**	7.5	40.9	51.6	**2.44**
19. Low HR/employee ratio	9.2	16.3	38.8	23.5	12.2	**3.13**	14.9	47.9	37.2	**2.22**
20. Low cost of HR services	3.1	19.6	39.2	28.8	11.3	**3.24**	7.5	40.9	51.6	**2.44**
21. Data-based talent strategy	19.4	27.6	27.6	16.3	9.2	**2.68**	6.4	37.2	56.4	**2.50**
22. Partner with line in developing business strategy	9.3	16.5	22.7	36.1	15.5	**3.32**	3.2	24.5	72.3	**2.69**
23. A human capital strategy that is integrated with business strategy	7.1	21.4	30.6	23.5	17.3	**3.22**	5.2	17.7	77.1	**2.72**
24. Provides analytic support for business decision-making	15.3	17.3	37.8	19.4	10.2	**2.92**	6.4	34.0	59.6	**2.53**
25. Provides HR data to support change management	5.2	23.7	34.0	23.7	13.4	**3.16**	4.3	36.6	59.1	**2.55**
26. HR drives change management	7.2	12.4	30.9	37.1	12.4	**3.35**	4.2	27.4	68.4	**2.64**
27. Makes rigorous data based decisions about human capital management	16.5	20.6	41.2	17.5	4.1	**2.72**	4.3	39.4	56.4	**2.52**

15. **A.** How has the amount of focus or attention to the following HR activities changed over the past 5 –7 years as a proportion of the overall Human Resource activity and emphasis?
(1 = Greatly Decreased, 3 = Stayed the Same, 5 = Greatly Increased)
   B. Have any of these activities been partially or completely outsourced?
(1 = Not At All, 2 = Partially, 3 = Completely)

| | | **A.** ACTIVITY AND EMPHASIS? | | | | | **B.** OUTSOURCING? | | | |
		Greatly Decreased	Stayed the Same	Greatly Increased	MEAN	Not At All	Partially	Completely	MEAN
a.	HR Planning	0	1.0	19.2	44.4	35.4	**4.14**	95.8	4.2	0	**1.04**
b.	Compensation	0	2.0	26.5	45.9	25.5	**3.95**	60.4	39.6	0	**1.40**
c.	Benefits	1.0	0	24.5	46.9	27.6	**4.00**	11.2	76.5	12.2	**2.01**
d.	Organization Development	1.0	8.2	24.5	39.8	26.5	**3.83**	77.9	22.1	0	**1.22**
e.	Organization Design	0	11.2	32.7	40.8	15.3	**3.60**	88.5	11.5	0	**1.11**
f.	Strategic Planning	1.0	3.1	17.7	50.0	28.1	**4.01**	92.6	7.4	0	**1.07**
g.	Employee Training/Education	2.0	9.1	24.2	42.4	22.2	**3.74**	24.0	76.0	0	**1.76**
h.	Management Development	1.0	5.1	17.3	42.9	33.7	**4.03**	45.3	53.7	1.1	**1.56**
i.	Union Relations	5.7	13.8	59.8	13.8	6.9	**3.02**	85.5	13.3	1.2	**1.16**
j.	HR Information Systems	0	2.0	23.5	43.9	30.6	**4.03**	55.3	40.4	4.3	**1.49**
k.	Performance Appraisal	0	3.0	27.3	45.5	24.2	**3.91**	90.5	8.4	1.1	**1.11**
l.	Recruitment	0	5.1	29.3	46.5	19.2	**3.80**	43.3	55.7	1.0	**1.58**
m.	Selection	0	3.0	31.3	48.5	17.2	**3.80**	76.3	23.7	0	**1.24**
n.	Career Planning	1.0	14.1	47.5	28.3	9.1	**3.30**	87.5	12.5	0	**1.13**
o.	Employee Record Keeping	6.1	16.2	52.5	20.2	5.1	**3.02**	59.4	33.3	7.3	**1.48**
p.	Legal Affairs	0	6.1	60.2	29.6	4.1	**3.32**	43.3	51.5	5.2	**1.62**
q.	Affirmative Action	1.0	12.2	59.2	25.5	2.0	**3.15**	67.4	26.3	6.3	**1.39**
r.	Employee Assistance	0	16.2	61.6	18.2	4.0	**3.10**	12.2	28.6	59.2	**2.47**
s.	Competency/Talent Assessment	2.0	5.1	28.3	43.4	21.2	**3.77**	56.8	37.9	5.3	**1.48**
t.	Data Analysis and Mining	0	4.0	42.4	45.5	8.1	**3.58**	82.3	15.6	2.1	**1.20**
u.	HR Metrics	0	6.1	28.3	44.4	21.2	**3.81**	86.5	11.5	2.1	**1.16**

Appendixes

16. **To what extent have you encountered the following problems in managing HR outsourcing/vendors?**

	(1 = Little or No Extent, 2 = Some Extent, 3 = Moderate Extent, 4 = Great Extent, 5 = Very Great Extent)	Little or No Extent	Some Extent	Moderate Extent	Great Extent	Very Great Extent	MEAN
a.	Resources required to manage the contract and relationship have been more than anticipated	20.6	22.7	37.1	14.4	5.2	**2.61**
b.	Services haven't been as good as promised..........	17.5	32.0	30.9	14.4	5.2	**2.58**
c.	Contractors don't know enough about the company	22.4	33.7	27.6	14.3	2.0	**2.40**
d.	Cost has been higher than promised	29.6	26.5	26.5	14.3	3.1	**2.35**
e.	Lack of skills for managing contractors	30.6	30.6	19.4	16.3	3.1	**2.31**
f.	Loss of competitive advantage from the way we manage people..	64.3	16.3	14.3	4.1	1.0	**1.61**
g.	Negative reaction from business units served........	37.8	34.7	15.3	10.2	2.0	**2.04**
h.	Negative reaction from company employees	33.3	34.4	20.8	9.4	2.1	**2.13**
i.	Negative reaction from HR employees...................	33.0	37.1	20.6	7.2	2.1	**2.08**
j.	Can't have HR systems we need	40.2	30.9	12.4	12.4	4.1	**2.09**
k.	Switch to new outsourcers is very difficult.............	25.8	25.8	27.8	16.5	4.1	**2.47**

17. **Please check the one statement that best describes the current state of your HR Information Technology.**

    1.   Completely integrated HR information technology system......................................**13.1%**

    2.   Most processes are information technology–based but not fully integrated **48.5%**

    3.   Some HR processes are information technology–based **32.3%**

    4.   Little information technology present in the HR function **6.1%**

    5.   No information technology present (GO TO QUESTION 19)............................... **0%**

18. **A.** **Can the following activities be done on your company's information technology system by employees and/or managers?** *(1 = Not At All, 2 = Partially, 3 = Completely)*

    B. **How effectively are these being done on your system?**
    (N/A = Not Applicable; 1 = Not Effective, 2 = Somewhat Effective, 3 = Very Effective)

    NOTE: Percentages and means for Section B are computed with N/A (Not Applicable) responses missing.

		A. IT System?				B. Effectiveness?				
		Not At All	Partially	Completely	MEAN	Not Applicable	Not Effective	Somewhat Effective	Very Effective	MEAN
a.	Salary and reward planning/administration...............	20.2	46.5	33.3	**2.13**	22.0	4.0	58.7	37.3	**2.33**
b.	Career development planning.....	44.0	49.0	7.0	**1.63**	47.0	21.2	67.3	11.5	**1.90**
c.	Change benefit coverage............	14.1	21.2	64.6	**2.51**	15.0	2.4	33.7	63.9	**2.61**
d.	Change address and/or other personal information	19.0	18.0	63.0	**2.44**	21.0	0.0	28.2	71.8	**2.72**
e.	Apply for a job (external applicants)	9.0	35.0	56.0	**2.47**	10.0	2.2	55.1	42.7	**2.40**
f.	Apply for a job (internal applicants)	8.1	25.3	66.7	**2.59**	9.0	2.2	52.8	44.9	**2.43**

18. **A.** **Can the following activities be done on your company's information technology system by employees and/or managers?** *(1 = Not At All, 2 = Partially, 3 = Completely)*

B. **How effectively are these being done on your system?**
(N/A = Not Applicable; 1 = Not Effective, 2 = Somewhat Effective, 3 = Very Effective)

NOTE: Percentages and means for Section B are computed with N/A (Not Applicable) responses missing.

		A. IT System?				B. Effectiveness?				
		Not At All	Partially	Completely	MEAN	Not Applicable	Not Effective	Somewhat Effective	Very Effective	MEAN
g.	Obtain advice and information on handling personnel issues	40.0	54.0	6.0	**1.66**	42.0	8.9	89.3	1.8	**1.93**
h.	Performance management	32.3	41.4	26.3	**1.94**	35.0	8.1	67.7	24.2	**2.16**
i.	Post job openings	9.1	27.3	63.6	**2.55**	11.0	4.7	49.4	45.9	**2.41**
j.	New hire orientation	39.4	54.5	6.1	**1.67**	40.0	7.0	75.4	17.5	**2.11**
k.	Skills training.............................	19.4	72.4	8.2	**1.89**	22.0	4.0	68.0	28.0	**2.24**
l.	Scheduling training	21.2	38.4	40.4	**2.19**	23.0	6.8	49.3	43.8	**2.37**
m.	Management development/ training..	35.4	61.6	3.0	**1.68**	38.0	10.2	74.6	15.3	**2.05**
n.	Search for employees with specified skills/competencies......	46.5	44.4	9.1	**1.63**	50.0	25.0	60.4	14.6	**1.90**
o.	Purchase products and services from vendors.................	29.9	52.6	17.5	**1.88**	31.1	4.7	75.0	20.3	**2.16**
p.	Post personal resume/bio	39.6	31.3	29.2	**1.90**	42.0	18.9	54.7	26.4	**2.08**
q.	Assess skills/ competencies/ knowledge.................................	41.4	48.5	10.1	**1.69**	44.0	24.5	66.0	9.4	**1.85**
r.	Access knowledge communities or experts...............	54.5	36.4	9.1	**1.55**	57.0	17.5	70.0	12.5	**1.95**
s.	Access managers' tool kit	35.4	44.8	19.8	**1.84**	36.0	5.0	73.3	21.7	**2.17**

19. **To what extent do you consider your eHR system to …**

	(1 = Little or No Extent, 2 = Some Extent, 3 = Moderate Extent, 4 = Great Extent, 5 = Very Great Extent)	Little or No Extent	Some Extent	Moderate Extent	Great Extent	Very Great Extent	MEAN
a.	Be effective	6.1	27.3	40.4	25.3	1.0	**2.88**
b.	Satisfy your employees	8.2	37.8	34.7	18.4	1.0	**2.66**
c.	Improve HR services...	8.1	22.2	33.3	32.3	4.0	**3.02**
d.	Build employee loyalty	36.4	31.3	25.3	6.1	1.0	**2.04**
e.	Reduce HR transaction costs...	7.1	29.6	26.5	25.5	11.2	**3.04**
f.	Alienate employees...	44.9	40.8	11.2	2.0	1.0	**1.73**
g.	Provide new strategic information	33.7	26.5	20.4	19.4	0	**2.26**
h.	Support strategic change	31.6	23.5	22.4	20.4	2.0	**2.38**
i.	Speed up HR processes	5.1	21.4	27.6	38.8	7.1	**3.21**
j.	Reduce the number of employees in HR	24.0	24.0	27.1	19.8	5.2	**2.58**
k.	Integrate HR processes (e.g., training, compensation)......	28.1	24.0	32.3	13.5	2.1	**2.38**
l.	Measure HR's impact on the business.............................	37.1	25.8	26.8	9.3	1.0	**2.11**
m.	Produce a dashboard or scorecard of HR's effectiveness...	39.2	27.8	18.6	11.3	3.1	**2.11**
n.	Enable analysis of workforce characteristics....................	21.1	30.5	25.3	18.9	4.2	**2.55**
o.	Provide a competitive advantage	32.3	33.3	21.9	9.4	3.1	**2.18**

20. How SATISFIED are you with the skills and knowledge of your organization's current HR professional/ managerial staff in each of these areas?

	(1 = Very Dissatisfied, 2 = Dissatisfied, 3 = Neutral, 4 = Satisfied, 5 = Very Satisfied)	Very Dissatisfied	Dissatisfied	Neutral	Satisfied	Very Satisfied	MEAN
a.	Team skills	1.0	4.1	26.5	56.1	12.2	3.74
b.	HR technical skills	0	5.1	17.3	48.0	29.6	4.02
c.	Business understanding	1.0	13.3	41.8	37.8	6.1	3.35
d.	Interpersonal skills	0	2.0	13.3	59.2	23.5	4.08
e.	Cross-functional experience	5.2	25.8	43.3	21.6	4.1	2.94
f.	Consultation skills	1.0	12.2	36.7	40.8	9.2	3.45
g.	Record keeping	1.0	4.1	33.7	48.0	13.3	3.68
h.	Coaching and facilitation	3.1	8.2	35.7	39.8	13.3	3.52
i.	Leadership/management skills	1.0	8.2	39.8	40.8	10.2	3.51
j.	Managing contractors/vendors	4.1	11.2	41.8	37.8	5.1	3.29
k.	Global understanding	7.2	32.0	41.2	16.5	3.1	2.76
l.	Organization design	5.1	20.4	40.8	30.6	3.1	3.06
m.	Strategic planning	5.1	28.6	35.7	25.5	5.1	2.97
n.	Information technology	3.1	22.4	46.9	23.5	4.1	3.03
o.	Change management	1.0	21.4	34.7	36.7	6.1	3.26
p.	Metrics development	7.1	42.9	30.6	15.3	4.1	2.66
q.	Data analysis and mining	8.2	37.8	26.5	23.5	4.1	2.78
r.	Communications	1.0	2.0	32.7	48.0	16.3	3.77
s.	Process execution and analysis	1.0	12.4	36.1	38.1	12.4	3.48

21. What percentage of your company-wide professional/managerial HR staff possess the necessary skill set for success in today's business environment? (Circle one)   **Mean = 4.50**

0%	2.1%	12.4%	37.1%	34.0%	11.3%	3.1%
(1)	(2)	(3)	(4)	(5)	(6)	(7)
None	Almost None	Some	About Half	Most	Almost All	All
0%	1-20%	21-40%	41-60%	61-80%	81-99%	100%

22. Does your organization currently …

(1 = Yes, Have Now, 2 = Being Built, 3 = Planning For, 4 = Not Currently Being Considered)	Yes, Have Now	Being Built	Planning For	Not Currently Being Considered	MEAN
a. Collect metrics that measure the business impact of HR programs and processes?	30.3	25.3	27.3	17.2	**2.31**
b. Collect metrics that measure the cost of providing HR services?	41.4	25.3	21.2	12.1	**2.04**
c. Have the capability to conduct cost-benefit analyses (also called utility analyses) of HR programs?	28.3	17.2	30.3	24.2	**2.51**
d. Use dashboards or scorecards to evaluate HR's performance?	39.4	23.2	23.2	14.1	**2.12**
e. Measure the financial efficiency of HR operations (e.g. cost-per-hire, time-to-fill, training costs?)	47.5	24.2	19.2	9.1	**1.90**
f. Have metrics and analytics that reflect the effects of HR programs on the workforce (such as, competence, motivation, attitudes, behaviors, etc.)?	29.3	25.3	27.3	18.2	**2.34**
g. Use measures and analytics to evaluate and track the performance of outsourced HR activities?	37.8	14.3	24.5	23.5	**2.34**
h. Benchmark analytics and measures against data from outside organizations (e.g., Saratoga, Mercer, Hewitt, etc.)?	48.5	15.2	25.3	11.1	**1.99**

23. How effective are the information, measurement, and analysis systems of your organization when it comes to:

(1 = Very Ineffective, 2 = Ineffective, 3 = Somewhat Effective, 4 = Effective, 5 = Very Effective)	Very Ineffective	Ineffective	Somewhat Effective	Effective	Very Effective	MEAN
a. Connecting human capital practices to organizational performance	10.1	30.3	50.5	8.1	1.0	**2.60**
b. Making decisions and recommendations that reflect your company's competitive situation	5.1	20.2	44.4	28.3	2.0	**3.02**
c. Identifying where talent has the greatest potential for strategic impact	4.0	22.2	49.5	21.2	3.0	**2.97**
d. Assessing HR programs before they are implemented – not just after they are operational	10.1	28.3	40.4	20.2	1.0	**2.74**
e. Pinpointing HR programs that should be discontinued	6.1	30.3	46.5	14.1	3.0	**2.78**
f. Assessing the feasibility of new business strategies	13.1	31.3	35.4	18.2	2.0	**2.65**
g. Evaluating the effectiveness of most HR programs and practices	3.1	20.4	52.0	23.5	1.0	**2.99**
h. Supporting organizational change efforts	3.0	11.1	45.5	35.4	5.1	**3.28**
i. Assessing and improving the HR department operations	0	10.2	40.8	44.9	4.1	**3.43**
j. Assessing and improving the human capital strategy of the company	2.0	26.5	43.9	23.5	4.1	**3.01**
k. Contributing to decisions about business strategy and human capital management	2.0	33.3	37.4	23.2	4.0	**2.94**

Appendixes

24. To what extent are these statements true about your organization?

(1 = Little or No Extent, 2 = Some Extent, 3 = Moderate Extent, 4 = Great Extent, 5 = Very Great Extent)	Little or No Extent	Some Extent	Moderate Extent	Great Extent	Very Great Extent	MEAN
a. Business leaders' decisions that depend upon or affect human capital (e.g., layoffs, rewards, etc.) are as rigorous, logical, and strategically relevant as their decisions about resources such as money, technology, and customers	6.2	22.7	28.9	35.1	7.2	**3.14**
b. Business leaders understand and use sound principles when making decisions about:						
1. Motivation..	6.1	33.3	27.3	31.3	2.0	**2.90**
2. Development and Learning...............................	7.1	29.3	37.4	22.2	4.0	**2.87**
3. Labor Markets	6.1	27.6	37.8	25.5	3.1	**2.92**
4. Culture..	5.1	22.2	40.4	27.3	5.1	**3.05**
5. Organizational Design...........................	5.1	24.2	39.4	29.3	2.0	**2.99**
6. Business Strategy	1.0	10.1	26.3	48.5	14.1	**3.65**
c. HR leaders identify unique strategy insights by connecting human capital issues to business strategy..	5.1	16.3	48.0	24.5	6.1	**3.10**
d. HR leaders have a good understanding about where and why human capital makes the biggest difference in their business	2.0	15.3	39.8	35.7	7.1	**3.31**
e. Business leaders have a good understanding about where and why human capital makes the biggest difference in their business	4.1	25.8	40.2	26.8	3.1	**2.99**

25. How much does your Corporation's Board call on HR for help with ...

(1 = Little or No Extent, 2 = Some Extent, 3 = Moderate Extent, 4 = Great Extent, 5 = Very Great Extent)	Little or No Extent	Some Extent	Moderate Extent	Great Extent	Very Great Extent	MEAN
a. Executive compensation	4.1	5.1	7.1	31.6	52.0	**4.22**
b. Addressing strategic readiness	19.2	24.2	22.2	25.3	9.1	**2.81**
c. Executive succession	4.0	14.1	18.2	29.3	34.3	**3.76**
d. Change consulting..	23.5	22.4	34.7	13.3	6.1	**2.56**
e. Developing board effectiveness/corporate governance..	33.3	20.2	21.2	17.2	8.1	**2.47**
f. Risk assessment	27.3	28.3	29.3	12.1	3.0	**2.35**
g. Information about the condition/capability of the work force	10.1	10.1	37.4	27.3	15.2	**3.27**
h. Board compensation	18.4	17.3	7.1	24.5	32.7	**3.36**

26. Please rate the activities on a scale of 1 to 10 by circling the appropriate number. If NOT APPLICABLE, circle N/A.

In view of what is needed by your company:

a. How *well* is the HR organization meeting needs in each of the areas below?
b. How important is it that HR do these well?

Note: Percentages and Mean are computed with N/A (Not Applicable) responses missing.

A. PROVIDING HR SERVICES

		1	2	3	4	5	6	7	8	9	10		N/A	MEAN
a	Not Meeting Needs	0	0	1.0	1.0	1.0	3.1	28.9	43.3	16.5	5.2	All Needs Met	0.0	7.79
b	Not Important	0	0	0	0	1.1	2.1	4.3	23.4	30.9	38.3	Very Important	1.0	8.96

B. PROVIDING CHANGE CONSULTING SERVICES

		1	2	3	4	5	6	7	8	9	10		N/A	MEAN
a	Not Meeting Needs	0	2.1	5.2	7.2	11.3	23.7	20.6	17.5	10.3	2.1	All Needs Met	0	6.45
b	Not Important	0	0	2.1	1.0	4.2	7.3	11.5	18.8	34.4	20.8	Very Important	0	8.23

C. BEING A BUSINESS PARTNER

		1	2	3	4	5	6	7	8	9	10		N/A	MEAN
a	Not Meeting Needs	0	0	4.1	2.1	10.3	11.3	29.9	25.8	14.4	2.1	All Needs Met	0	7.06
b	Not Important	0	0	0	1.0	2.1	1.0	9.4	12.5	26.0	47.9	Very Important	0	9.00

D. IMPROVING DECISIONS ABOUT HUMAN CAPITAL

		1	2	3	4	5	6	7	8	9	10		N/A	MEAN
a	Not Meeting Needs	0	0	3.1	7.2	15.5	17.5	23.7	20.6	8.2	4.1	All Needs Met	0	6.67
b	Not Important	0	2.1	1.0	2.1	0	3.1	13.5	29.2	19.8	29.2	Very Important	0	8.32

E. TAILORING HUMAN RESOURCE PRACTICES TO FIT BUSINESS NEEDS

		1	2	3	4	5	6	7	8	9	10		N/A	MEAN
a	Not Meeting Needs	0	1.0	4.1	5.2	5.2	15.5	22.7	22.7	20.6	3.1	All Needs Met	0	7.10
b	Not Important	0	1.0	1.0	0	2.1	3.1	16.7	24.0	26.0	26.0	Very Important	0	8.38

F. HELPING SHAPE A VIABLE EMPLOYMENT RELATIONSHIP FOR THE FUTURE

		1	2	3	4	5	6	7	8	9	10		N/A	MEAN
a	Not Meeting Needs	2.1	1.1	2.1	4.3	9.6	16.0	21.3	25.5	16.0	2.1	All Needs Met	2.0	6.89
b	Not Important	0	0	0	0	2.2	3.2	10.8	31.2	24.7	28.0	Very Important	2.0	8.57

26. Please rate the activities on a scale of 1 to 10 by circling the appropriate number. If NOT APPLICABLE, circle N/A.

In view of what is needed by your company:

a. How *well* is the HR organization meeting needs in each of the areas below?
b. How important is it that HR do these well?

Note: Percentages and Mean are computed with N/A (Not Applicable) responses missing.

(continued)

G. MANAGING OUTSOURCING OF TRANSACTIONAL SERVICES (e.g. BENEFITS)

		1	2	3	4	5	6	7	8	9	10		N/A	MEAN
a	Not Meeting Needs	0	1.1	2.2	5.6	5.6	13.5	15.7	22.5	23.6	10.1	All Needs Met	8.0	7.44
b	Not Important	0	1.1	0	2.3	5.7	9.1	21.6	22.7	17.0	20.5	Very Important	8.0	7.85

H. MANAGING OUTSOURCING OF HR EXPERTISE (e.g. COMPENSATION DESIGN)

		1	2	3	4	5	6	7	8	9	10		N/A	MEAN
a	Not Meeting Needs	1.4	0	2.7	4.1	12.2	20.3	9.5	18.9	21.6	9.5	All Needs Met	23.0	7.15
b	Not Important	1.4	1.4	0	1.4	16.2	8.1	18.9	21.6	16.2	14.9	Very Important	22.0	7.39

I. OPERATING HR CENTERS OF EXCELLENCE

		1	2	3	4	5	6	7	8	9	10		N/A	MEAN
a	Not Meeting Needs	0	2.3	5.7	3.4	9.1	17.0	21.6	27.3	9.1	4.5	All Needs Met	9.0	6.80
b	Not Important	0	0	1.1	2.2	6.7	7.9	23.6	22.5	23.6	12.4	Very Important	7.0	7.74

J. OPERATING HR SHARED SERVICE UNITS

		1	2	3	4	5	6	7	8	9	10		N/A	MEAN
a	Not Meeting Needs	0	1.1	3.4	5.7	10.3	18.4	18.4	29.9	6.9	5.7	All Needs Met	10.0	6.85
b	Not Important	1.1	0	3.4	2.3	5.7	10.3	21.8	20.7	16.1	18.4	Very Important	9.0	7.59

K. HELPING TO DEVELOP BUSINESS STRATEGIES

		1	2	3	4	5	6	7	8	9	10		N/A	MEAN
a	Not Meeting Needs	1.1	2.1	7.4	12.6	10.5	21.1	22.1	17.9	3.2	2.1	All Needs Met	1.0	6.04
b	Not Important	0	0	0	2.1	6.4	8.5	18.1	24.5	16.0	24.5	Very Important	1.0	8.02

L. BEING AN EMPLOYEE ADVOCATE

		1	2	3	4	5	6	7	8	9	10		N/A	MEAN
a	Not Meeting Needs	2.1	1.1	1.1	3.2	7.4	10.5	14.7	32.6	17.9	9.5	All Needs Met	0	7.40
b	Not Important	1.1	0	2.1	1.1	6.3	9.5	17.9	21.1	17.9	23.2	Very Important	0	7.86

26. Please rate the activities on a scale of 1 to 10 by circling the appropriate number. If NOT APPLICABLE, circle N/A.

In view of what is needed by your company:

a. How *well* is the HR organization meeting needs in each of the areas below?
b. How important is it that HR do these well?

Note: Percentages and Mean are computed with N/A (Not Applicable) responses missing.

(continued)

M. ANALYZING HR AND BUSINESS METRICS

		1	2	3	4	5	6	7	8	9	10		N/A	MEAN
a	Not Meeting Needs	1.1	5.3	11.7	8.5	11.7	19.1	20.2	13.8	4.3	4.3	All Needs Met	0	5.88
b	Not Important	0	1.1	2.1	2.1	3.2	5.3	16.0	30.9	23.4	16.0	Very Important	0	7.94

N. WORKING WITH THE CORPORATE BOARD

		1	2	3	4	5	6	7	8	9	10		N/A	MEAN
a	Not Meeting Needs	2.2	4.5	3.4	1.1	9.0	10.1	13.5	27.0	19.1	10.1	All Needs Met	5.0	7.15
b	Not Important	1.1	2.2	0	3.4	7.9	6.7	6.7	21.3	20.2	30.3	Very Important	5.0	8.02

O. OVERALL PERFORMANCE

		1	2	3	4	5	6	7	8	9	10		N/A	MEAN
a	Not Meeting Needs	0	1.1	0	2.1	7.4	13.7	25.3	43.2	6.3	1.1	All Needs Met	0	7.19
b	Not Important	0	0	0	0	1.1	3.2	7.5	20.4	32.3	35.5	Very Important	2.0	8.86

We need you to do one more thing. Please let us know who you gave the executive survey to. We will only use this information to follow-up with them. We will not report any individual responses.

(1) Name: _____

   Title: _____

   Phone: (   ) _____ Email: _____

(2) Name: _____

   Title: _____

   Phone: (   ) _____ Email: _____

(3) Name: _____

   Title: _____

   Phone: (   ) _____ Email: _____

The Practice of Human Resource Management:
A Survey of Executives Not in the HR Function
Item Report (N = 77, Aggregated)

1. **Which of the following best describes the relationship between the Human Resource function and the business strategy of your corporation? (Please check one response)**

    1. Human Resource plays no role in business strategy **(GO TO QUESTION 2)**..............................**5.3%**

    2. Human Resource is involved in implementing the business strategy......................................**18.4%**

    3. Human Resource provides input to the business strategy and helps
        implement it once it has been developed...**52.6%**

    4. Human Resource is a full partner in developing and implementing the business strategy. **23.7%**

ANSWER QUESTIONS 1a, ONLY IF YOU CHECKED 2, 3, OR 4 FOR QUESTION 1 above.

1a. **Please respond to the following questions by circling one number in each row. With respect to strategy, to what extent does the HR function …**

(1 = Little or No Extent, 2 = Some Extent, 3 = Moderate Extent, 4 = Great Extent, 5 = Very Great Extent)	Little or No Extent	Some Extent	Moderate Extent	Great Extent	Very Great Extent	MEAN
a. Help identify or design strategy options	9.5	28.4	41.9	20.3	0.0	**2.70**
b. Help decide among the best strategy options	6.8	21.6	48.6	17.6	5.4	**2.86**
c. Help plan the implementation of strategy	0.0	10.8	43.2	33.8	12.2	**3.42**
d. Help design the criteria for strategic success	8.1	18.9	41.9	27.0	4.1	**2.94**
e. Help identify new business opportunities	31.1	35.1	28.4	5.4	0.0	**2.04**
f. Assess the organizations readiness to implement strategies	1.4	8.1	45.9	28.4	16.2	**3.43**
g. Help design the organization structure to implement strategy	2.7	10.8	28.4	43.2	14.9	**3.50**
h. Assess possible merger, acquisition, or divestiture strategies	20.8	43.1	16.7	15.3	4.2	**2.33**
i. Work with the corporate board on business strategy	21.6	28.4	29.7	17.6	2.7	**2.46**
j. Recruit and develop talent	0.0	2.7	8.1	45.9	43.2	**4.20**

2. **How SATISFIED are you with the skills and knowledge of your organization's current HR professional/managerial staff in each of these areas?**

(1 = Very Dissatisfied, 2 = Dissatisfied, 3 = Neutral, 4 = Satisfied, 5 = Very Satisfied)	Very Dissatisfied	Dissatisfied	Neutral	Satisfied	Very Satisfied	MEAN
a. Team skills	1.3	0.0	19.5	57.1	22.1	**3.89**
b. HR technical skills	1.3	1.3	10.4	54.5	32.5	**4.10**
c. Business understanding	0.0	7.8	36.4	48.1	7.8	**3.47**
d. Interpersonal skills	0.0	3.9	11.7	51.9	32.5	**4.04**
e. Cross-functional experience	1.3	15.8	40.8	36.8	5.3	**3.23**

2. How SATISFIED are you with the skills and knowledge of your organization's current HR professional/managerial staff in each of these areas?

(1 = Very Dissatisfied, 2 = Dissatisfied, 3 = Neutral, 4 = Satisfied, 5 = Very Satisfied)	Very Dissatisfied	Dissatisfied	Neutral	Satisfied	Very Satisfied	MEAN
f. Consultation skills	0.0	7.8	27.3	49.4	15.6	3.68
g. Record keeping	1.3	7.8	26.0	44.2	20.8	3.69
h. Coaching and facilitation	2.6	6.5	20.8	55.8	14.3	3.64
i. Leadership/management skills	5.2	3.9	26.0	50.6	14.3	3.57
j. Managing contractors/vendors	0.0	6.5	41.6	49.4	2.6	3.39
k. Global understanding	2.6	10.5	39.5	44.7	2.6	3.30
l. Organization design	1.3	6.6	31.6	47.4	13.2	3.61
m. Strategic planning	1.3	15.6	40.3	39.0	3.9	3.19
n. Information technology	2.6	13.0	55.8	24.7	3.9	3.09
o. Change management	1.3	5.2	28.6	51.9	13.0	3.60
p. Metrics development	0.0	15.6	45.5	32.5	6.5	3.25
q. Data analysis and mining	2.6	16.9	53.2	26.0	1.3	3.03
r. Communications	0.0	6.6	14.5	60.5	18.4	3.81
s. Process execution and analysis	0.0	6.5	31.2	50.6	11.7	3.61

3. What percentage of your company-wide professional/managerial HR staff possess the necessary skill set for success in today's business environment? (Circle one)   Mean = 4.33

0%	5.3%	17.1%	27.6%	36.8%	13.2%	0%
None	Almost None	Some	About Half	Most	Almost All	All
0%	1-20%	21-40%	41-60%	61-80%	81-99%	100%

4. To what extent are these statements true about your organization?

(1 = Little or No Extent, 2 = Some Extent, 3 = Moderate Extent, 4 = Great Extent, 5 = Very Great Extent)	Little or No Extent	Some Extent	Moderate Extent	Great Extent	Very Great Extent	MEAN
a. Business leaders' decisions that depend upon or affect human capital (e.g., layoffs, rewards, etc.) are as rigorous, logical, and strategically relevant as their decisions about resources such as money, technology, and customers	1.3	11.7	31.2	40.3	15.6	3.52
b. Business leaders understand and use sound principles when making decisions about:						
1. Motivation	2.6	19.5	35.1	39.0	3.9	3.13
2. Development and Learning	2.6	15.6	35.1	37.7	9.1	3.26
3. Labor Markets	1.3	13.0	48.1	32.5	5.2	3.18
4. Culture	0.0	15.8	34.2	39.5	10.5	3.36
5. Organizational Design	2.6	9.1	41.6	39.0	7.8	3.28
6. Business Strategy	1.3	5.2	28.6	57.1	7.8	3.54
c. HR leaders identify unique strategy insights by connecting human capital issues to business strategy	3.9	14.3	50.6	24.7	6.5	3.06
d. HR leaders have a good understanding about where and why human capital makes the biggest difference in their business	0.0	7.8	26.0	53.2	13.0	3.62
e. Business leaders have a good understanding about where and why human capital makes the biggest difference in their business	0.0	13.0	39.0	42.9	5.2	3.37

5. **Please rate the activities on a scale of 1 to 10 by circling the appropriate number. If NOT APPLICABLE, circle N/A.**

In view of what is needed by your company:

a. How *well* is the HR organization meeting needs in each of the areas below?

b. How important is it that HR do these well?

Note: Percentages and Mean are computed with N/A (Not Applicable) responses missing.

A. PROVIDING HR SERVICES

		1	2	3	4	5	6	7	8	9	10		N/A	MEAN
a	Not Meeting Needs	0.0	0.0	3.9	3.9	5.2	10.4	26.0	33.8	14.3	2.6	All Needs Met	0.0	7.18
b	Not Important	0.0	1.3	1.3	0.0	0.0	0.0	7.8	16.9	36.4	36.4	Very Important	0.0	8.80

B. PROVIDING CHANGE CONSULTING SERVICES

		1	2	3	4	5	6	7	8	9	10		N/A	MEAN
a	Not Meeting Needs	1.3	3.9	6.5	5.2	15.6	18.2	28.6	11.7	7.8	1.3	All Needs Met	2.6	6.09
b	Not Important	0.0	0.0	1.3	0.0	3.9	6.5	19.5	19.5	31.2	18.2	Very Important	1.3	8.11

C. BEING A BUSINESS PARTNER

		1	2	3	4	5	6	7	8	9	10		N/A	MEAN
a	Not Meeting Needs	1.3	3.9	5.2	1.3	10.4	10.4	23.4	20.8	19.5	3.9	All Needs Met	0.0	6.79
b	Not Important	0.0	0.0	0.0	0.0	0.0	1.3	7.8	23.4	44.2	23.4	Very Important	0.0	8.75

D. IMPROVING DECISIONS ABOUT HUMAN CAPITAL

		1	2	3	4	5	6	7	8	9	10		N/A	MEAN
a	Not Meeting Needs	0.0	6.5	1.3	3.9	3.9	18.2	33.8	14.3	18.2	0.0	All Needs Met	0.0	6.67
b	Not Important	0.0	0.0	0.0	0.0	0.0	1.3	9.1	19.5	41.6	28.6	Very Important	0.0	8.80

E. TAILORING HUMAN RESOURCE PRACTICES TO FIT BUSINESS NEEDS

		1	2	3	4	5	6	7	8	9	10		N/A	MEAN
a	Not Meeting Needs	1.3	3.9	2.6	1.3	16.9	20.8	23.4	19.5	10.4	0.0	All Needs Met	0.0	6.37
b	Not Important	0.0	0.0	0.0	0.0	0.0	5.2	11.7	20.8	40.3	22.1	Very Important	0.0	8.55

F. HELPING SHAPE A VIABLE EMPLOYMENT RELATIONSHIP FOR THE FUTURE

		1	2	3	4	5	6	7	8	9	10		N/A	MEAN
a	Not Meeting Needs	0.0	6.5	2.6	3.9	5.2	22.1	24.7	24.7	9.1	1.3	All Needs Met	3.9	6.51
b	Not Important	0.0	0.0	0.0	1.3	1.3	2.6	5.2	23.4	42.9	23.4	Very Important	3.9	8.61

G. MANAGING OUTSOURCING OF TRANSACTIONAL SERVICES (e.g., BENEFITS)

		1	2	3	4	5	6	7	8	9	10		N/A	MEAN
a	Not Meeting Needs	0.0	0.0	2.8	2.8	15.3	15.3	23.6	18.1	15.3	6.9	All Needs Met	19.5	6.94
b	Not Important	0.0	0.0	0.0	0.0	4.2	20.8	18.1	20.8	23.6	12.5	Very Important	19.5	7.71

5. Please rate the activities on a scale of 1 to 10 by circling the appropriate number. If NOT APPLICABLE, circle N/A.

In view of what is needed by your company:

a. How *well* is the HR organization meeting needs in each of the areas below?
b. How important is it that HR do these well?

Note: Percentages and Mean are computed with N/A (Not Applicable) responses missing.

(continued)

H. MANAGING OUTSOURCING OF HR EXPERTISE (e.g., COMPENSATION DESIGN)

		1	2	3	4	5	6	7	8	9	10		N/A	MEAN
a	Not Meeting Needs	0.0	3.0	3.0	4.5	12.1	18.2	21.2	18.2	18.2	1.5	All Needs Met	33.8	6.69
b	Not Important	0.0	0.0	3.0	3.0	10.6	12.1	13.6	18.2	30.3	9.1	Very Important	32.5	7.43

I. OPERATING HR CENTERS OF EXCELLENCE

		1	2	3	4	5	6	7	8	9	10		N/A	MEAN
a	Not Meeting Needs	1.4	4.1	11.0	5.5	12.3	16.4	20.5	19.2	6.8	2.7	All Needs Met	28.6	6.04
b	Not Important	1.4	0.0	4.1	1.4	6.8	6.8	20.3	18.9	25.7	14.9	Very Important	27.3	7.56

J. OPERATING HR SHARED SERVICE UNITS

		1	2	3	4	5	6	7	8	9	10		N/A	MEAN
a	Not Meeting Needs	0.0	1.4	4.3	10.0	11.4	15.7	17.1	31.4	7.1	1.4	All Needs Met	32.5	6.50
b	Not Important	0.0	0.0	4.3	1.4	12.9	5.7	11.4	32.9	24.3	7.1	Very Important	29.9	7.41

K. HELPING TO DEVELOP BUSINESS STRATEGIES

		1	2	3	4	5	6	7	8	9	10		N/A	MEAN
a	Not Meeting Needs	0.0	7.9	5.3	13.2	15.8	19.7	19.7	10.5	6.6	1.3	All Needs Met	5.2	5.65
b	Not Important	0.0	0.0	1.3	3.9	9.2	13.2	22.4	25.0	13.2	11.8	Very Important	2.6	7.30

L. BEING AN EMPLOYEE ADVOCATE

		1	2	3	4	5	6	7	8	9	10		N/A	MEAN
a	Not Meeting Needs	0.0	2.6	1.3	1.3	9.1	6.5	29.9	19.5	20.8	9.1	All Needs Met	1.3	7.34
b	Not Important	0.0	1.3	0.0	2.6	2.6	7.8	19.5	24.7	22.1	19.5	Very Important	0.0	7.94

M. ANALYZING HR AND BUSINESS METRICS

		1	2	3	4	5	6	7	8	9	10		N/A	MEAN
a	Not Meeting Needs	1.3	3.9	0.0	11.7	16.9	9.1	29.9	11.7	13.0	2.6	All Needs Met	3.9	6.36
b	Not Important	0.0	0.0	0.0	1.3	2.6	3.9	16.9	32.5	31.2	11.7	Very Important	3.9	8.10

5. **Please rate the activities on a scale of 1 to 10 by circling the appropriate number. If NOT APPLICABLE, circle N/A.**

   In view of what is needed by your company:

   a. **How *well* is the HR organization meeting needs in each of the areas below?**
   b. **How important is it that HR do these well?**

   Note: Percentages and Mean are computed with N/A (Not Applicable) responses missing.

(continued)

N. WORKING WITH THE CORPORATE BOARD

		1	2	3	4	5	6	7	8	9	10		N/A	MEAN
a	Not Meeting Needs	0.0	4.4	4.4	4.4	7.4	11.8	14.7	26.5	14.7	11.8	All Needs Met	27.3	7.07
b	Not Important	0.0	0.0	0.0	2.9	4.4	7.4	16.2	22.1	26.5	20.6	Very Important	26.0	8.05

O. OVERALL PERFORMANCE

		1	2	3	4	5	6	7	8	9	10		N/A	MEAN
a	Not Meeting Needs	0.0	3.9	1.3	7.8	5.2	13.0	29.9	22.1	16.9	0.0	All Needs Met	0.0	6.73
b	Not Important	0.0	0.0	0.0	0.0	1.3	1.3	7.9	17.1	47.4	25.0	Very Important	3.9	8.75

6. **Where do you currently work (please select one):**

   1. General Management **51.3%**

   2. Production **14.5%**

   3. Marketing / Sales **11.8%**

   4. Finance / Accounting...........**13.2%**

   5. Technical / Engineering.........**2.6%**

   6. Other: _____ **6.6%**